The Uniform Business Rate
A Practical Guide

'ERSITY   RGAN

Tolley Publishing Company Limited

The Uniform Business Rate
A Practical Guide

Second Edition

by WJ McCluskey FRICS, ASVA, Dip Prop Inv
Senior Lecturer, University of Ulster

and PJ Moss FRICS, IRRV, Dip Arb, ACIArb
Partner, Richard Ellis

Tolley Publishing Company Limited
un A United News & Media publication

ISBN 1 86012 050-4

First published 1992
Second edition March 1996

Published by
Tolley Publishing Company Limited
Tolley House
2 Addiscombe Road
Croydon
Surrey
CR9 5AF
0181 686 9141

© 1996 WJ McCluskey and PJ Moss
Typeset in Great Britain by
Action Typesetting Limited, Northgate Street, Gloucester

Printed and bound in Great Britain by
BPC Books and Journals Ltd

Preface

Since the first edition of this book in 1992 considerable changes have taken place in the treatment of domestic and non-domestic properties within the area of local government finance. The Community Charge in all its forms was abolished, and in its place residential property became liable to the Council Tax (with effect from 1 April 1993).

The law and practice of non-domestic rating has continued to develop since the 1990 general revaluation. Significant changes have resulted in the following areas: appeal procedures, rights of appeal, time limits, effective dates, the role of the Valuation Tribunal (formerly the Valuation and Community Charge Tribunal), transitional relief, and composite hereditaments, to list but a few.

The aim of the authors in producing this second edition has been to try and incorporate the most important and significant changes to the law in a manner which is both logical and constructive. Those involved with rating matters still have to contend with a proliferation of statutory instruments. We hope that the structure of this book provides the reader with a transparent and simple guide through this maze of SIs.

The structure of this new edition follows that of the original book, with chapters devoted to alterations and appeals, rating lists, transitional relief, unoccupied property, billing and collection and so forth.

The authors have continued to endeavour to present the material in a way which can be readily understood by the intended readership of general practice and rating surveyors, finance directors, company secretaries and students. Although it is difficult with a topic as complex as this not to expect the reader to have some prior knowledge of the subject, we hope that those unfamiliar with the subject will obtain ready answers to their questions.

The authors gratefully acknowledge the assistance and suggestions in compiling this second edition from friends and acquaintances in private practice, billing authorities, Valuation Tribunals and the Valuation Office Agency.

Special thanks are also due to the Valuation Office Agency for kind permission to reproduce material in the Appendix.

William McCluskey
Peter Moss
March 1996

All royalties from this book have been donated by the authors to the Royal Institution of Chartered Surveyors Benevolent Fund.

Contents

Table of Statutes

Table of Statutory Instruments

Table of Cases

Chapter 1

Rating lists

Relevant legislation:

- Local Government Finance Act 1988;
- Local Government and Housing Act 1989;
- Non-Domestic Rating (Miscellaneous Provisions) Regulations 1989 (SI 1989 No 1060);
- Non-Domestic Rating (Miscellaneous Provisions) (No 2) Regulations 1989 (SI 1989 No 2303) as amended;
- Non-Domestic Rating (Miscellaneous Provisions) (No 2) (Amendment) Regulations 1993 (SI 1993 No 544);
- Central Rating Lists Regulations 1994 (SI 1994 No 3121).

Before the Local Government Finance Act 1988, the old system of business rating was based on the valuation list, which was essentially a detailed record of hereditaments and assessments within the area of a local authority. It dated back to the Union Assessment Committee Act 1862, which provided for the compilation of the valuation list, and which also provided that no poor rate should be levied unless the hereditament appeared in the list.

'Hereditament' is the unit of property which is liable for assessment to non-domestic rating. Although hereditament is not specifically defined in the Local Government Finance Act 1988, section 64 does expressly provide for the continuing use of the definition contained in section 115(1) of the General Rate Act 1967, where hereditament is defined as '... property which is or may become liable to a rate, being a unit of such property which is or would fall to be shown as a separate item in the valuation list'. Each hereditament forms a separate entry in the rating list, having its own description and assessment.

Under the new legislation, the assessment is then multiplied by the uniform business rate which is equivalent to the old rate in the pound as previously determined by the local authorities. The multiplier is fixed by the Secretary of State for the Environment and is applied uniformly throughout England (a separate multiplier is set for Wales) upon all non-domestic properties irrespective of the type of property.

The Local Government Finance Act 1988 ('LGFA 1988') has replaced the valuation list with two new lists:

- local non-domestic rating list (s 41);
- central non-domestic rating list (s 52).

The level of information contained in the new lists is broadly the same as was contained in the valuation list. Of interest, however, is the introduction of the central rating list, which contains entries only for properties occupied by various designated statutory undertakers.

The Green Paper, *Paying for Local Government*, which was published in January 1986, expressed the Government's belief that it was essential to return to regular revaluations in the non-domestic sector; and section 41(2) of the LGFA 1988 now provides for regular revaluations at five-yearly intervals. This contrasts markedly with the previous haphazard track record of revaluations (1956, 1963, 1973). Section 68 of the General Rate Act 1967 provided for the making of new valuation lists at regular intervals, to be specified by the Secretary of State subject to confirmation by Parliament; the first new list was to be in 1978 but this and other review dates were postponed by Parliament. One hopes that '1 April 1990 and on 1 April in every fifth year afterwards' reflects the Government's intention, rather than mere optimism. To some extent this early optimism is approaching reality, given that the 1990 revaluation has now been followed by one in 1995, with the Government committed to undertake a further revaluation in the year 2000. It would at best be premature to forecast beyond the year 2000, but at least the track record for five-yearly revaluations will be in place along with the substantive experience of the Valuation Office Agency in undertaking them.

1. Local non-domestic rating list

It is the responsibility of the valuation officer for a billing authority to compile and maintain the local rating list. The valuation officer has custody of the list; previously this responsibility lay with the rating authority. The list comes into force on the day on which it is compiled, i.e. 1 April 1995 for the current list, and remains in force until superseded by a later list. The valuation officer must take sufficient steps to ensure that on 1 April the list has been accurately prepared. In compiling and maintaining the list, the valuation officer may take into account information obtained under his powers to call for returns and to enter premises; these powers were contained in sections 82 and 86 of the General Rate Act 1967, and have been re-enacted in Schedule 9 (paras 5 and 6) to the LGFA 1988.

At any time between depositing the draft list on 31 December (see page 4) and its coming into force three months later on 1 April, the valuation officer can on his own initiative alter the list. Since the draft list will have been made on the information available to the valuation officer up until 31 December, the list can be altered to reflect new information or representations. Any alterations made to the draft list must be notified to the billing authority or the Secretary of State.

(a) Contents

Details on the contents of local lists are prescribed in section 42 of the LGFA 1988 and in the Non-Domestic Rating (Miscellaneous Provisions) Regulations 1989 (SI 1989 No 1060).

For each day in each chargeable financial year the list must show every hereditament which:

- is situated in the authority's area;
- is a relevant non-domestic hereditament;
- is at least partly neither domestic property nor exempt from non-domestic rating (exempt properties, as listed in Schedule 5 to the LGFA 1988, include agricultural property, places of public religious worship, parks); and
- is not one which would be shown in the central non-domestic rating list.

For each day the list must also show whether the hereditament consists entirely of property which is not domestic or that it is a composite hereditament (with 'part' being added to the description), and whether any part of the hereditament is exempt. The list must show for each day the rateable value of the hereditament, or the rateable value of the non-domestic part or non-exempt part.

Additional information which is contained in the list includes:

- the description of the hereditament;
- its address; and
- any reference number ascribed to it by the valuation officer.

With regard to alterations made to the list, the list must show the date on which the last alteration took effect and must state if the alteration was at the direction of the Valuation Tribunal or the Lands Tribunal.

2. Central non-domestic rating list

Although the vast majority of rateable hereditaments are included in the local non-domestic rating lists, section 52 of the LGFA 1988 provides for the compilation of a central rating list by the central valuation officer. It came into force on 1 April 1990 and remained in force until 1 April 1995 when a new list superseded it.

As soon as a new list has been compiled, the central valuation officer must send a copy to the Secretary of State who deposits it at his principal office. The central rating list will show for a designated person a single aggregate rateable value for hereditaments of a prescribed description, or, as the case may be, the value for a single hereditament. The rates levied on the aggregate value or single hereditament are paid to the Secretary of State who then pays them into the national non-domestic rate pool. The intention behind the establishment of these lists is that they should contain only those properties occupied by statutory undertakers and national networks, with a view to securing *en bloc* rating of such properties. This change from the previous system simplifies procedures, particularly where a hereditament, such as pipelines or cables, is spread over numerous charging authority boundaries, thus avoiding the need for special rules relating to apportionment of rateable values.

Two central non-domestic rating lists are compiled and maintained – one for England, and the other for Wales.

(a) Contents

Section 53 of the LGFA 1988 details the contents of the central list. It must show for each day in each year for which the list is in force:

- the name of each designated person; and
- against the name each hereditament situated in England which on the day concerned is occupied, or if unoccupied is owned, by that person.

Against each name are also shown:

- where the person is a registered company, its registered office and in any other case the person's principal place of business in the United Kingdom;
- where the person is a registered company, its registered number;

- the first day, if later than 1 April 1995, for which the rateable value shown in the list had effect;
- if the rateable value has been altered by a tribunal, the name of the tribunal;
- the total of the rateable value shown in the list.

(Central Rating Lists Regulations 1994 (SI 1994 No 3121).)

Under section 53(1) of the LGFA 1988, the Secretary of State may by regulations designate a person and prescribe in relation to him one or more descriptions of relevant non-domestic hereditaments, and any information about the hereditaments (s 53(5)). A designated person's name cannot be removed from the central rating list except by the amendment of the appropriate regulations.

(b) Statutory prescription of rateable values

The practice of prescribing rateable values of certain public utilities began in the 1950s to overcome various technical problems associated with the assessment of these undertakings by conventional methods. The present power to prescribe rateable values is contained in paragraph 3 of Schedule 6 to the LGFA 1988. The majority of ratepayers covered by central rating are already subject to specific arrangements which recognise the regional or national nature of their operation. The Government is committed to a policy of ending the practice of prescribed assessment in as many instances as possible. However, it has not been possible at this stage (1995) because of the practical difficulties involved in collecting and processing the kind of information required. It is likely that by the year 2000 as many industries as is practicable will return to conventional assessment. The following industries for the present remain under the prescribed assessment rules: water supply industry, British Railways Board, Railtrack plc, London Underground and statutory docks and harbours with receipts of £1m and above.

Several industries have now reverted to conventional assessment, including British Telecommunications, Mercury Communications, British Waterways Board, Docklands Light Railway, Tyne and Wear Metro and statutory docks and harbours with relevant receipts of less than £1m.

At the revaluation in 1990, the prescribed industries had their rateable values set by reference to the net book value of the rateable assets as shown in the undertaking's current cost accounts. After making any necessary allowance for disabilities (such as the age or lay-out of buildings, or their technical or functional obsolescence), the resultant value is similar to the effective capital value; this is then converted to an annual value by the application of a decapitalisation rate, which has been prescribed at 5.5 per cent (see para 2(5) Non-Domestic Rating (Miscellaneous Provisions) (No 2) (Amendment) Regulations (SI 1994 No 3122)). For water, gas and electricity undertakings, this has proved to be a reliable and consistent approach. For those undertakers where the net book value cannot be determined, the valuation method involves taking a percentage of the undertaking's turnover.

For the 1995 revaluation the Government has used the 1994/95 rateable values as the basis for the new list rateable values. However, since the antecedent valuation date (AVD) – 1 April 1993 – certain industries have been subject to major changes and new values have had to be determined. To take British Rail and Railtrack as an example, because of major changes in the rail industry since the AVD the values for both companies are drawn from the British Railways Board's adjusted turnover for Great Britain in the financial year 1992/93. Adjustments were made for the value of separately assessed offices, separately rated subsidiaries and subsequently privatised enterprises. The rateable value for the whole of Great Britain has then been apportioned between England, Scotland and Wales on the basis of operational activity in each country and then divided between the two companies in the ratio in which they occupy the property: 95:5 for Railtrack and British Rail respectively in England and 97:3 in Wales.

There are also rules governing the annual updating of a rateable value in accordance with changes in the level of activity of the undertaking. This is calculated by reference to a predetermined yardstick for each industry which is deemed to reflect changes in the value of the hereditaments described in the list. This recalculation can result in either an increase or decrease in the rateable value.

Where transitional relief applies to a central list entry whose value has been prescribed, the relief is built into the assessment which changes annually as a result not only of the activity level but also of the phasing brought about by transition. Thus the ratepayer will always be liable to pay rates at the appropriate multiplier on the full rateable value in the list.

It has been decided that the British Waterways Board will not be entitled to transitional relief, because a substantial proportion of the Board's properties are assessed by conventional means and are entered in local lists.

Cross-country pipelines appearing in the central list are valued conventionally; as with local list hereditaments, any transitional relief is applied at the billing stage.

Statutory docks and harbours are entitled to transitional relief whether or not they are valued by formula (there is a minimum level of income below which the Order does not apply – SI 1989 No 2473).

(c) Excepted hereditaments

With regard to the specified statutory undertakers, 'excepted hereditaments' do not appear in the central rating list, but rather in the local non-domestic rating lists. Excepted hereditaments tend to be those hereditaments, like shops, which are located in typical retail locations (such as electricity and gas showrooms) and offices not situated on operational land. For each undertaker, such excepted hereditaments are specifically defined in the relevant regulations.

In *Halliday (VO) v British Railways Board* [1994] RA 297, the question arose of whether a railway booking office should be entered in the local rating list as being an excepted (from the central list) hereditament, because it was premises used wholly or mainly as offices not situated on operational land. Operational land is defined as meaning land which is used for the purposes of carrying on that person's undertaking, not being land which, in respect of its nature and situation, is comparable rather with land in general than with land which is used for the purposes of carrying on statutory undertakings. The subject property was contained in a shopping centre adjacent to a railway station. The Lands Tribunal followed its earlier decision in *British Railways Board v Westminster City Council and Mattey* [1972] RA 373 in holding that ticket offices were office premises. The subject being in a situation similar to that of shops in a modern shopping centre, the Tribunal held that the ticket office was, in respect of its nature and situation, comparable more with land in general rather than land used for the purposes of a statutory undertaking, and was therefore not situated on operational land of the Board.

3. Alterations of rateable values

Where a rateable value has been prescribed, a ratepayer may make a proposal to alter the list at any time.

There are two distinct groups of regulations governing appeals against entries in the central list. Those applying to pipelines are essentially the same as those which apply to local list hereditaments, with minimal changes in wording; those applying to the remaining entries, resulting from prescribed assessments, are slightly different. It is the responsibility of the relevant valuation officer in maintaining the list to make any revision required by application of an updating factor. The ratepayer has a right of appeal against the alteration. Any dispute can be referred to the Valuation Tribunal in the normal way (see Chapter 3). However, the Valuation Tribunal does not have jurisdiction to question or revise the values or rules laid down in the statutory instruments; its concern is limited to the application of the rules in each case.

4. Prescribed assessment examples

With regard to formula rating, the LGFA 1988 opens the way to the valuation of undertakings on a conventional basis. The intention of the Government is, as far as practicable, to return all hereditaments whose values are currently prescribed to conventional assessment for the year 2000.

With reference to the 1995 revaluation, however, and in particular the valuation of public utilities, where previously the rateable value of a hereditament occupied by a public utility undertaking was estimated solely by reference to the accounts or profits of the undertaking, the Non-Domestic Rating (Miscellaneous Provisions) (No 2) Regulations 1989 now provide that all available evidence relevant to estimating the amount of rent in accordance with paragraph 2(1), (1A) or (1B) of Schedule 6 to the LGFA 1988 is taken into account. Sub-paragraphs (1A) and (1B) were inserted by paragraph 38(4) of Schedule 5 to the Local Government and Housing Act 1989, and overrule the precedent establised in *Kingston Union Assessment Committee v Metropolitan Water Board* [1926] AC 331.

Under paragraph 3 of Schedule 6 to the LGFA 1988, the Secretary of State has the power to prescribe rateable values, or to determine the rateable value in accordance with prescribed rules. To date a number of such orders have been made. They include:

- British Gas plc (Rateable Values) Order 1989 (SI 1989 No 2471);
- Docks and Harbours (Rateable Values) Order 1989 (SI 1989 No 2473) as amended;
- Telecommunications Industry (Rateable Values) Order 1989 (SI 1989 No 2478);
- Non-Domestic Rating (Railways) and Central Rating Lists (Amendment) Regulations 1994 (SI 1994 No 834);
- Telecommunications Industry (Rateable Values) (Amendment) Order 1994 (SI 1994 No 903);
- Central Rating Lists Regulations 1994 (SI 1994 No 3121);
- Non-Domestic Rating (Railways, Telecommunications and Canals) Regulations 1994 (SI 1994 No 3123);
- Docks and Harbours (Rateable Values) (Amendment) Order 1994 (SI 1994 No 3280);

- British Waterways Board and Telecommunications Industry (Rateable Values) Revocation Order 1994 (SI 1994 No 3281);
- Electricity Supply Industry (Rateable Values) Order 1994 (SI 1994 No 3282);
- British Gas plc (Rateable Values) Order 1994 (SI 1994 No 3283);
- Railways (Rateable Values) Order 1994 (SI 1994 No 3284);
- Water Undertakers (Rateable Values) Order 1994 (SI 1994 No 3285);
- Electricity Supply Industry (Rateable Values) Order 1995 (SI 1995 No 962).

(a) British Gas plc

The valuation formula for the central list entry is contained in the British Gas plc (Rateable Values) Order 1994 (SI 1994 No 3283).

The rateable values have been calculated as at 1 April 1995, by reference to the 1994/95 list entry, to which an adjustment (if any) has been made. These adjustments are to reflect the changes brought about by the recalculation factor.

For the year beginning 1 April 1995, £483,887,500 was specified as the rateable value of gas hereditaments situated in England.

Changes for 1995/96 and subsequent years are determined by changes in the length of regional and national transmission mains, by reference to the following formula:

$$T \left(\frac{y - Y}{Y} \right)$$

where: T is the prescribed rateable value;
   Y is the estimated length of relevant pipeline in the country on 31 March 1995;
   y is the estimated length of relevant pipeline in the country on 31 March in the preceding year.

(b) Water undertakers (water supply industry)

The valuation formula for the central list entry is contained in the Water Undertakers (Rateable Values) Order 1994 (SI 1994 No 3285).

The rateable values for the prescribed water supply undertakers have been calculated using the 1994/95 list entries as a base. Values subsequent to 1 April 1995 can be adjusted by applying a recalculation factor.

(c) Electricity supply industry

The valuation formula for the central list entry is set out in the Electricity Supply Industry (Rateable Values) Order 1994 (SI 1994 No 3282).

The rateable values as at 1 April 1995 for hereditaments of the electricity supply industry have been calculated using 1994/95 list values. Adjustments to these values have been made to reflect changes in generating capacity, transmission line or transformer capacity as at 31 March 1995.

(i) Electricity generating hereditaments

National Power plc
PowerGen plc
Nuclear Electric plc

For the annual recalculation of rateable values, the formula to be applied is:

$$\text{£}11,620 \, (D-d)$$

where: £11,620 is the rateable value per megawatt of declared net capacity
(£16,426 per megawatt for Nuclear Electric plc)
D is the total declared net capacity of generating plant on 31 March in the relevant preceding year
d is the total declared net capacity of generating plant on 31 March 1995.

Certain hereditaments not occupied by National Power plc, PowerGen plc and Nuclear Electric plc will have their assessments entered in local rating lists. This is provided that the following conditions are met:

- the Primary function of the hereditament is for the purpose of generating electricity; and
- the primary source of energy is the burning of refuse; or
- the generating plant uses wind, tidal or water power as its primary source of energy; or
- has a declared net capacity of 500 kilowatts or more (25 megawatts or more in the case of those hereditaments whose source of energy is the burning of refuse).

The rateable value is calculated by reference to the following formula:

£5,810 rateable value per megawatt of net capacity for wind or tidal power; or

£11,620 rateable value per megawatt of net capacity in all other cases.

(ii) Electricity transmission hereditaments

National Grid Company plc

For the annual recalculation of rateable values, the formula to be applied is:

$$T \left(\frac{k - K}{K} \right)$$

where: T   is the amount specified in relation to that class in the schedule, i.e. the prescribed rateable value

   k   is the estimated number of circuit kilometres of main transmission line on 31 March in the relevant preceding year

   K   is the number of main transmission line in kilometres as at 31 March 1995.

(iii) Electricity distribution

Eastern Group plc

East Midlands Electricity plc

London Electricity plc

Manweb plc

Northern Electric plc

Norweb plc

SEEBOARD plc

Scottish Power plc

Southern Electric plc

South Wales Electricity plc

South Western Electricity plc

Yorkshire Electricity Group plc

The recalculation factor is determined by reference to the following formula:

$$T \left(\frac{v - V}{V} \right)$$

11

where: T is the specified rateable value

v is the transformer capacity on 31 March in the relevant preceding year

V is the transformer capacity on 31 March 1995.

(d) Statutory docks and harbours

The rateable value is calculated on a basis similar to that laid down in the Docks and Harbours (Rateable Value) Order 1976 (SI 1976 No 535). The value is a specified percentage of the relevant income of the port. The definition of income has been amended to include cargo handling, but continues to exclude pilotage receipts and certain investment income. The relevant income for valuation purposes is approximately 90 per cent of the total turnover.

Where the hereditament is located in more than one billing authority area, regulations provide that there will be only one list entry in the local non-domestic rating list for the authority with the greatest area of the hereditament. There will accordingly be one rates bill payable by the undertaker.

The Government has considered that the approach adopted for the assessment of rateable values under the previous 1990 revaluation was satisfactory and has found no need to change it. The accounts for year 1992/93 will be used as the base for calculating the 1 April 1995 rateable value. The rateable value will represent 9 per cent of the relevant income.

The Docks and Harbours (Rateable Values) (Amendment) Order 1994 (SI 1994 No 3280), which amends the 1989 Order (SI 1989 No 2473), prescribes the rules for the calculation of rateable values for docks and harbours with relevant receipts over £1m as at 1 April 1993. This has the effect that for those docks and harbours whose relevant receipts are less than £1m, conventional rating assessment will apply.

(e) Railways

The valuation formula is contained in the Railways (Rateable Values) Order 1994 (SI 1994 No 3284).

The prescribed rateable values as at 1 April 1995 are as follows:

 (i)   in the case of the English railway hereditament occupied by Railtrack plc, £206,114,100;

 (ii) in the case of the English railway hereditament occupied by the British Railways Board, £10,848,100;

 (iii) in the case of the London Underground hereditaments, £44,600,000.

In each subsequent year, the rateable value of each hereditament shall be the amount produced in respect of that year by applying the standard formula in relation to the hereditaments. The standard formula is given by:

$$T + U$$

where: T   is the rateable value for the year beginning on 1 April 1995

U   is the recalculation factor.

The recalculation factor is determined in accordance with the formula for Railtrack plc and the British Railways Board:

$$\frac{2P + F}{3}$$

where: F   is the figure calculated by reference to:

$$\frac{g - G}{G}$$

where: g   is the estimated annual average number of millions of net tonne-kilometres of revenue-earning freight carried on the railways of the relevant designated person in the period of three years ending on 31 March in the relevant preceding year

G   is the estimated annual average number of millions of net tonne-kilometres of revenue-earning freight carried on those railways in the period of three years ending on 31 March 1995

P   is the figure calculated in accordance with:

$$\frac{j - J}{J}$$

where: j   is the estimated annual average number of millions of passenger kilometres undertaken on the railways of the relevant designated person in the period of three years ending on 31 March in the relevant preceding year

J   is the estimated annual average number of such passenger kilometres in the period of three years ending on 31 March 1995.

It should now be noted that hereditaments occupied by the Docklands Light Railway Ltd and the Tyne and Wear Passenger Transport Executive are to be conventionally assessed but remain included within the central rating list.

(f) British Waterways Board

The Non-Domestic Rating (Railways, Telecommunications and Canals) Regulations 1994 (SI 1994 No 3123) provide that more than one hereditament should be treated as one hereditament (reg 5(2)) if occupied by or, if unoccupied, owned by the British Waterways Board. Such property can include the following: waterways, aqueducts, lighthouses, docks, wharves, piers, jetties, clay pits and other land and buildings not comprised in an excepted hereditament.

The British Waterways Board and Telecommunications Industry (Rateable Values) Revocation Order 1994 (SI 1994 No 3281) provides that hereditaments whose rateable values were specified or determined in accordance with the rules set out in the British Waterways Board (Rateable Values) Order 1989 (SI 1989 No 2472) will, with effect from 1 April 1995, be assessed under the normal rules of valuation for rating and entered in the central rating list.

(g) Telecommunications

Telecommunications includes the following designated persons:

British Telecommunications plc;
Mercury Communications Ltd;
BR Telecommunications Ltd;
Energis Communications Ltd;
AT&T (UK) Ltd.

The British Waterways Board and Telecommunications Industry (Rateable Values) Revocation Order 1994 (SI 1994 No 3281) provides that, with effect from 1 April 1995, all properties occupied by British Telecommunications plc and Mercury Communications Ltd will be assessed under the normal rules of valuation for rating.

(h) Long distance pipelines

Though not public utility undertakings, cross-country pipelines tend to be located across more than one billing authority, and are properly included in the central rating list. A list of designated persons is contained in the Central Rating Lists Regulation 1994 (SI 1994 No 3121).

There are no prescribed rateable values and no statutory formula laid down to determine the rateable values. Therefore a conventional approach is to be adopted.

Chapter 2

Alterations to the rating list

Relevant legislation:

- Local Government Finance Act 1988;
- Local Government and Housing Act 1989;
- Non-Domestic Rating (Payment of Interest) Regulations 1990 (SI 1990 No 1904) (as amended);
- Non-Domestic Rating (Alteration of Lists and Appeals) Regulations 1993 (SI 1993 No 291);
- Non-Domestic Rating (Alteration of Lists and Appeals) (Amendment) Regulations 1994 (SI 1994 No 1809);
- Non-Domestic Rating (Alteration of Lists and Appeals) (Amendment) Regulations 1995 (SI 1995 No 609).

The Local Government and Finance Act 1988 replaced the term 'valuation list', which was used in the General Rate Act 1967, with the terms 'local non-domestic rating list' and 'central non-domestic rating list'. This reflected the significant change in the function of the list. Under section 43 of the LGFA 1988, the list became conclusive on almost all matters concerning liability to pay rates in respect of a hereditament. All exemptions from rating are now given effect by exclusion from the local or central rating lists. The lists must show not only any changes in rateable value but also the date from which such changes take effect, i.e. the effective date. If it wants to, the billing authority may keep and maintain a separate 'shadow list'. Any alterations made to the rating lists by the valuation officer are notified to the billing authority – so it can then update its 'shadow' list.

All references to regulations in this chapter are to the 1993 Regulations (SI 1993 No 291), unless otherwise indicated.

1. Alteration of draft lists

With regard to the local non-domestic rating list and the central non-domestic rating list, the valuation officer is required to deposit for public inspection drafts of the lists not later than 31 December, i.e. three months before the new lists come into force. Ratepayers were not individually notified of their rateable values in advance of the coming into force of the 1990 lists. This was changed for the 1995 lists, and ratepayers are now given notice of their draft entry. In effect this follows the long-established practice in Scotland. Alterations to the draft lists during the period between their deposit in draft and the coming into force of the compiled lists in April are largely informal, as there has been no re-enactment of section 68 of the General Rate Act 1967. There is no right of appeal at this stage.

Valuation officers can make alterations of their own volition if new information comes to light. A ratepayer and a billing authority can make representations to the valuation officer which may lead him to alter the list. Where the list is altered, the valuation officer must notify the billing authority or the Secretary of State (depending on whether the alteration is to the local list or to the central list) who will then alter their copies. It is the list compiled on 1 April that determines liability from that date.

2. Local rating lists

Once a list has come into force, it may be altered for any of the reasons specified in regulation 4A of the 1993 Regulations (SI 1993 No 291):

(a) the rateable value shown in the list for a hereditament was inaccurate on the day the list was compiled;

(b) the rateable value shown in the list for a hereditament is inaccurate by reason of a material change of circumstances which occurred on or after the day on which the list was compiled;

(c) the rateable value shown in the list for a hereditament by reason of an alteration made by a valuation officer is or has been inaccurate;

(d) the rateable value or any other information shown in the list for a hereditament is shown, by reason of a decision in relation to another hereditament of a valuation tribunal, the Lands Tribunal or a court determining an appeal or application for review from either such tribunal, to be or to have been inaccurate;

(e) the day from which an alteration is shown in the list as having effect is wrong;

(f) a hereditament not shown in the list ought to be shown in that list;

(g) a hereditament shown in the list ought not to be shown in that list;

(h) the list should show that some part of a hereditament which is shown in the list is domestic property or is exempt from non-domestic rating but does not do so;

(i) the list should not show that some part of a hereditament which is shown in the list is domestic property or is exempt from non-domestic rating but does so;

(j) property which is shown in the list as more than one hereditament ought to be shown as one or more different hereditaments;

(k) property which is shown in the list as one hereditament ought to be shown as more than one hereditament;

(l) the address shown in the list for a hereditament is wrong;

(m) the description shown in the list for a hereditament is wrong; and

(n) any statement required to be made about the hereditament under section 42 of the Act has been omitted from the list.

The coming into force of a new list limits the ability to make alterations to the previous list. Only some of the above reasons will be valid and, even then, will be subject to strict time limits.

The following may cause the rating list to be altered:

(i) the valuation officer;

(ii) the billing authority (in limited cases only, unless acting in its capacity as an occupier or owner of an interest (i.e. 'an interested person'));

(iii) an 'interested person'.

(a) Alteration of the rating list by the valuation officer

Under the General Rate Act 1967 ('the old system') the valuation officer was obliged to serve a proposal to alter the list, whereas under the 1988 Act there is no such requirement. He may alter the rating list at any time as part of his general duty to maintain the list.

However, within four weeks of altering the list, the valuation officer must serve notice on the relevant billing authority stating the effect of the alteration. No later than the day on which that notice is served, he must also notify the ratepayer and any current proposer, stating the effect of such alteration, its effective date, and rights of appeal (reg 18(2) – as amended).

Notification of alteration under regulation 18(2) does not apply to alterations effected solely as a result of: (i) the correction of a clerical error, (ii) the decision of the valuation officer that a proposal is well founded, (iii) agreed alterations under regulation 11, (iv) a change in the address of the hereditament, (v) changes in the area of a billing authority or (vi) decisions of the Valuation Tribunal or the Lands Tribunal.

(b) Proposals by the billing authority

Under the old system, the rating authority could make proposals to alter the list, mainly to reflect the inclusion of new hereditaments and/or increases in rateable values following alterations and extensions to buildings.

Under the LGFA 1988, and the principal regulations (SI 1993 No 291), a billing authority, unless acting as a ratepayer or an interested person, may only make a proposal to alter a rating list where:

(i)   a material change in circumstances after the date of compilation of the list has resulted in an inaccurate rateable value being shown in the list; or

(ii)   as a result of a decision by a Valuation Tribunal or the Lands Tribunal on some other hereditament, the rateable value or some other information shown for a hereditament is inaccurate; or

(iii)   a hereditament shown in a list ought not to be shown, or a hereditament not shown ought to be shown; or

(iv)   a list should show some part of a hereditament as domestic or exempt, or it does show such qualification and should not do so.

(c) Interested person

Under the old system, the right to make a proposal was conferred (*inter alia*) on 'persons aggrieved'. Under the 1988 Act, a proposal to alter the local rating list is to be made by an 'interested person' who disagrees with the rateable value entered in the list or such other matters as are specified in regulation 4A of SI 1993 No 291.

Under regulation 2 of SI 1993 No 291, 'interested person' is defined as being the occupier and any other person owning an interest in the hereditament. That interest does not have to be the freehold; a leasehold or an agreement for the lease is sufficient. It extends to:

(a) any person (other than a mortgagee not in possession) having in any part of the hereditament either:

    (i) a legal estate, or

    (ii) an equitable interest such as would entitle him (after the cessation of any prior interest) to possession of the hereditament or any part of it; and

(b) any person having a qualifying connection with the occupier or with any person such as described in (a) above.

By regulation 2(2), category (b) above includes subsidiary and parent companies within a group. Additionally, a person who is not currently an interested person has the right to make a proposal if the value of a hereditament is altered or its effective date is amended for any period for which he was an interested person.

(d) When to make a proposal

For the 1990 rating lists, the right to make a proposal is very restricted after 1 April 1995. In essence, under regulation 4, proposals can only be made up to 31 March 1996 where a relevant authority or interested person is of the opinion that the 1990 list ('the old list') was inaccurate because:

    (i) a hereditament was shown in the list when it ought not to have been shown; or

    (ii) a hereditament was not shown when it ought to have been; or

    (iii) a list should have shown some part of a hereditament as domestic or exempt and did not do so, or it did show such qualification and should not have done; or

    (iv) one hereditament constituted two or more, or vice versa.

Additionally, an interested person may make a proposal up to six months after the date of a decision of a Valuation Tribunal or the Lands Tribunal – regulation 4(4) – or within six months of the alteration of the old list by the valuation officer – regulation 4(9).

For the 1995 and subsequent rating lists, under regulation 4B a proposal to alter a list compiled on or after 1 April 1995 may be made at any time before the first anniversary of the compilation of the next list. With quinquennial revaluations, proposals to alter the 1995 lists may be made at any time up to 31 March 2001.

The ability to make proposals may go beyond this first anniversary of the compilation of the next list. The circumstances are related to specific events, making it possible for proposals to be made up to one year after the event where this is later than the anniversary of the compilation of the next list. The specified events are:

(i)   alteration of the rateable value by the valuation officer;

(ii) a decision by a Valuation Tribunal or the Lands Tribunal in relation to another hereditament; or

(iii) a previous alteration which gave rise to an inaccuracy.

(e) How to make a proposal

Regulations 5 and 5A of the 1993 Regulations, as amended, set out the manner in which a proposal should be made and the information required to be included on such a document.

There is no prescribed form for the making of a proposal. However, the proposal must be made in writing, stating the name and address of the person making it, including their capacity for making it, and it must be served upon the valuation officer.

It must also identify the property to which it relates, and the manner in which it is proposed that the list be altered, e.g. by changing the rateable value, or deleting the entry from the list. The proposal will form the basis on which any subsequent appeal to the Valuation Tribunal or Lands Tribunal will be determined; it should therefore clarify the grounds on which the proposal is made and state any information required under the particular regulation.

A statement of reasons for believing the list to be incorrect, or the rateable value to be excessive, should be incorporated. If it is claimed that there has been a material change of circumstances, a statement is required specifying the nature of the change and the date on which the person making the proposal believes the change occurred.

If the proposal is made in response to the valuation officer's alteration, it should state the date on which the valuation officer issued the notice informing the ratepayer of the alteration. If the proposal disputes the day from which such an alteration should have effect, it should state an alternative date.

Under regulation 5(3) a proposal may deal with more than one hereditament only:

(i)   where it is contended that more than one hereditament shown in the list ought to be shown as one or more different hereditaments; or

(ii) where one hereditament is shown and it is contended that it constitutes more than one hereditament; or

(iii)   where the person making the proposal does so in the same capacity in relation to each hereditament, and each hereditament is within the same building or the same curtilage.

(f) Invalid proposals

If the valuation officer is of the opinion that a proposal has not been validly made, then under regulation 7 he may serve an invalidity notice on the proposer within four weeks of the proposal, stating why he considers it to be invalid. The maker of the proposal can then either appeal against the invalidity notice, by serving a notice of disagreement upon the valuation officer, or make a further proposal. This latter option will result in the original proposal being treated as having been withdrawn.

Under the old system there were a number of leading cases relating to the approach of the Lands Tribunal and the courts in construing proposals: *Behrmann v Seymour* [1972] RA 313; *Re Evans' Application* [1973] JPL 657; *Guest v Boughton* [1981] RA 97, (1981) 258 EG 68. It appears that the same general principles apply to the new system.

Although the requirements are fully set out in regulation 5A, it is worth noting an important case on the question of validity of proposals: *R v Winchester Area Assessment Committee, ex parte Wright* [1948] 2 KB 455. In that case Scott LJ stated:

> 'The proposal must give sufficient information to enable the assessment committee to know (1) whether an increase or decrease is asked for; (2) to which of the existing valuations in the (rating list) the proposal refers; (3) what is the ground of complaint as to the existing valuation on that point; and it is enough to state "incorrect or unfair" unless there is some unusual ground, in which case it ought to be specified'.

Similarly, the requirement to identify the hereditament to which the proposal relates does not appear to demand an exact description of the property, but rather an adequate identification of it. In the Court of Appeal case, *R v Northamptonshire Local Valuation Court, ex parte Anglian Water Authority* [1990] RA 93, an error in describing the address of a property was held to invalidate the proposal, with the consequence that the ratepayer paid rates for a substantial period of time which otherwise might not have been payable.

Until the validity of the proposal is finally decided on appeal to the Valuation Tribunal or the Lands Tribunal, the substantive appeal procedure under regulations 8–12 is suspended (reg 7(9)). It is therefore crucial that a great deal of care is taken in the initial preparation of the proposal.

(g) Withdrawal of proposals

Regulation 10 covers those circumstances in which a proposal can be withdrawn. Because the pursuance or non-pursuance of an appeal may affect subsequent appellants' rights, the circumstances in which a proposal may be withdrawn are expressly provided for. Thus, where a proposal has been made by a departed occupier, it may not be withdrawn except with the written agreement of the present occupier (reg 10(2)).

Additionally, there is a provision (reg 10(3)) under which an interested person may 'join in' a proposal made by another within two months of the making of that proposal. In such circumstances, where the original maker of the proposal subsequently withdraws, after receiving notice of that withdrawal from the valuation officer, the interested person can serve notice upon the valuation officer stating that he is aggrieved by the withdrawal of the proposal. Such notice will be treated as a proposal by that person made on the day he served his notice on the valuation officer.

In any other circumstances, the maker of a proposal is free to withdraw it. However, once the proposal has been referred to the tribunal, every party to the appeal, except the valuation officer, must signify their agreement to the withdrawal.

(h) Agreed alterations following proposals

Where the valuation officer and all parties agree in writing to an alteration to the list, the valuation officer must alter the list within two weeks of the date when agreement is reached, provided that it is not sooner than two months from the date when the proposal was served on the valuation officer (reg 11). The following must be parties to the written agreement:

- the valuation officer;
- the maker of the proposal;
- the ratepayer at the date of the proposal (unless he has moved away and cannot be traced);
- the ratepayer at the date of the agreement;
- any other interested person, or the relevant authority, who would have been competent to make the proposal in question.

Procedure for proposals for alteration

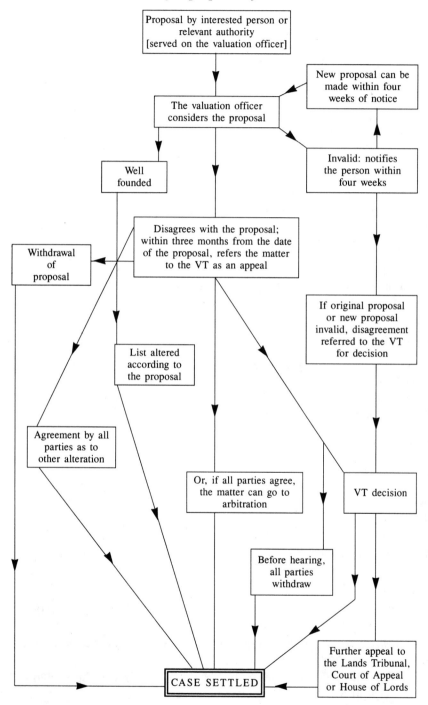

(i) *Disagreement on proposed alterations*

Where the valuation officer is of the opinion that a proposal is not well founded, and (i) it is not withdrawn, and (ii) no agreement has been reached, the disagreement must, no later than three months after the day on which the proposal was served, be referred by the valuation officer to the Valuation Tribunal as an appeal by the maker of the proposal (reg 12).

The valuation officer is required to send a statement of the following to the clerk of the tribunal:

- the entry (if any) in the list which it is proposed should be altered:
- the date of service of the proposal;
- the names and addresses of those persons who are required to be party to any written agreement on an alteration (if known);
- the grounds on which the proposal was made.

The valuation officer must also transmit to the clerk of the tribunal the name and address of any other person who has given notice that he wishes to be a party to the appeal.

(j) *Effective dates*

Rating lists must show the effective date of any alteration. An alteration in the amount a ratepayer is liable to pay takes effect from the date on which the list is deemed to have been altered. The provisions relating thereto are set out in regulations 13, 15, 16 and 44 of the 1993 Regulations and were significantly modified by the 1994 Regulations, particularly for alterations after 1 April 1992.

They are extremely complicated and are a good example of those pieces of legislative drafting which do not render up their true meaning very easily! Although a brief general outline follows, it is recommended that, in anything but the most straightforward case, the regulations themselves should be consulted.

(i) An alteration effected so as to show any hereditament, which, since the list was compiled:

    (a) has come into existence or has ceased to exist;

    (b) has ceased to be, or has become, domestic property exempt from non-domestic rating;

    (c) part of which has become, or has ceased to be, domestic property, or exempt;

    (d) has ceased to be, or has become, required to be shown in a central rating list; or

(e)   has ceased to be within or has become within, or forms part of the billing authority's area by virtue of a change in that area,

generally has effect from the day on which the circumstances giving rise to the alteration occurred.

(ii)   An alteration made so as to reflect any matter mentioned in paragraph 2(7) of Schedule 6 to the LGFA 1988, which covers the following:

(a)   matters affecting the physical state or physical enjoyment of the hereditament;

(b)   the mode or category of occupation of the hereditament;

(c)   the quantity of minerals or other substances in or extracted from the hereditament;

(cc)   the quantity of refuse or waste material which is brought on to and permanently deposited on the hereditament;

(d)   matters affecting the physical state of the locality in which the hereditament is situated, or which, though not affecting the physical state of the locality, are none the less physically manifest there; and

(e)   the use or occupation of other premises situated in the locality of the hereditament,

generally has effect from the day on which the circumstances giving rise to the alteration arose (reg 13(5)).

However, where this date is not ascertainable, because, for example, the change took place gradually over a long period of time, the following rules apply (reg 13(6)):

(a)   where the alteration is made in pursuance of a proposal, the alteration has effect from the day on which the proposal was served on the valuation officer;

(b)   in any other case the alteration has effect from the day on which it was entered in the list.

(iii)   Any alteration of a list, to give effect to a completion notice, can only have effect from the date specified in the notice. Where, under Schedule 4A, a different day is substituted by a subsequent notice, or agreed between the rated owner and the authority, or determined on appeal, the alteration will have effect from the date so substituted, agreed or determined.

The 1993 Regulations were significantly amended by the 1994 Regulations, particularly with respect to effective dates, as a response to the perceived need to close a loophole in the transitional arrangements – often referred to as the $^N/_J$ problem. However, in closing this loophole, the regulations have become extremely complex and have produced a situation where, for the first time, extensive back-dating of rate liabilities can result.

The occupier and owner have the right to make a proposal challenging the date specified in the rating list. Failing agreement with the valuation officer, the matter will be referred to the Valuation Tribunal for a decision.

3. Examples of effective dates

Example A: simple case

(i)   Entry in list 1.4.95: £25,000 rateable value;
(ii) Proposal served by occupier 1.9.95, seeking reduction to £20,000;
(iii) All-party agreement reached 21.6.96: £22,500 rateable value;
(iv) Valuation officer alters list 1.7.96 to £22,500 rateable value.

Result: £22,500 rateable value is effective from 1.4.95 and original and subsequent rate bills are recalculated accordingly.

Example B: later change in assessment

Following on from example A, the occupier demolishes part of his property on 1.2.97:

(i)   If he serves his proposal before 31.3.97, the altered value is effective from 1.2.97;
(ii) If, however, he does not serve his proposal until 1.6.97 albeit on the same grounds, the reduced value takes effect only from 1.4.97.

Example C: completion notices

(i)   Completion notice served by billing authority on 1.6.95 specifying 1.7.95 is appealed against by the owner within twenty-eight days;
(ii) Valuation officer alters list on 1.8.95 to include hereditament at £50,000 rateable value from 1.7.95;
(iii) Ratepayer serves proposal on 1.10.95 for a reduction and for a different effective date;
(iv) Effective date is subsequently agreed (or determined) as being 1.9.95. (This must be resolved before any appeal against the valuation officer's alteration is considered.);

(v)   All-party agreement reached on 1.6.96 at £45,000 rateable value, and with an effective date of 1.9.95;

(vi) Valuation officer alters list on 8.6.96.

Result: £45,000 rateable value is effective from 1.9.95, and empty property rates (see Chapter 4), if applicable, are payable from 1.12.95.

Note: Once a completion notice has been served and, if challenged, subsequently upheld, if the valuation officer does not alter the list until the following financial year, the effective date of the valuation officer's alteration is the date finally determined or agreed in respect of the completion notice, even though this is in an earlier financial year.

Example D: proposal following earlier alteration of list

(i)   Entry in list on 1.4.95 at £25,000 rateable value;

(ii) Valuation officer alters list on 30.11.95 to £30,000 rateable value (with an effective date of 30.9.95);

(iii) Occupier makes a proposal on 30.4.96 challenging the value at (ii) and the effective date;

(iv) All-party agreement reached on 30.10.96 at £28,500 and effective date of 30.10.95;

(v)   Valuation officer alters list on 7.11.96 to give effect to the value and dates at (iv) above.

Result: £25,000 rateable value is effective from 1.4.95 until 29.10.95 and £28,500 is effective from 30.10.95 onwards. Rate bills are recalculated accordingly.

4. Central rating lists

(a) Alteration of the rating list by the central valuation officer

As in the case of local rating lists, it is implicit that the central valuation officer maintains the central list once it has been compiled. There is a duty imposed by regulation 21 of SI 1993 No 291 on the central valuation officer to alter the list from time to time, whether prospectively or retrospectively, to conform with regulations under section 53 and relevant orders under paragraph 3(2) of Schedule 6 to the LGFA 1988.

An alteration may occur as a result of the application of the annual updating factors which are prescribed for those hereditaments which are included in the central rating list. Within four weeks of altering a central list, the central valuation officer must notify the designated person and the Secretary of State of the effect of the alteration. The Secretary of State must then alter the list held at his principal office.

Where an alteration is made, the list must show the day from which the alteration is to have effect.

(b) Proposals to alter the central list

Proposals may be made only by designated persons, and must be served upon the central valuation officer (reg 23). The person making the proposal must identify the hereditament in writing, and must refer to specific information, namely (i) the designated person's name and address, (ii) the rateable value proposed, (iii) a statement of the person's reasons for believing the list to be incorrect, and (iv) if the proposal seeks to change the effective date, the proposed date.

Within two weeks of the service on him, the central valuation officer must serve a copy on the appropriate Secretary of State. Where the central valuation officer considers a proposal to be well founded, he shall, as soon as reasonably practicable, alter the list accordingly.

Where the central valuation officer and the designated person agree in writing to an alteration other than that contained in the proposal, the valuation officer must within two weeks of such agreement alter the list, and the proposal is deemed to have been withdrawn.

Where the central valuation officer considers that a proposal is not well founded, and the proposal is not withdrawn, and no agreement has been reached, he must within three months of the date of service on him refer the disagreement to the relevant Valuation Tribunal, and such referral is deemed to be an appeal by the maker of the proposal.

5. Interest payable on rate refunds

The Non-Domestic Rating (Payment of Interest) Regulations 1990 (SI 1990 No 1904) (as amended) introduced a system entitling business ratepayers who challenge their assessments to receive interest for any delay in settling their challenge. If a retrospective reduction in the rateable value is awarded, simple interest will be paid on any sums overpaid pending the adjustment. Ratepayers will therefore not be penalised if there is a significant delay before appeals are settled.

Interest would thus be paid where, as a result of an alteration to the rating list – whether by the valuation officer, or by agreement with the valuation officer, or by an order of a tribunal – an assessment is reduced with an effective date earlier than the current financial year.

Liability is defined in the regulations as meaning:

- a person's liability under section 43 or section 45 of the 1988 Act (see SI 1991 No 2111), covering empty rates as well as occupied rates; and
- a person's liability under section 54 of the 1988 Act.

(a) Entitlement to interest

(i) Where, as a result of an alteration to a rating list, a person is entitled to a repayment, the billing authority or, as the case may be, the Secretary of State must pay or credit an additional amount by way of interest on the repayment.

(ii) Where a ratepayer has had a liability order or a judgment made against him, there is no entitlement to interest on the repayment.

However, the Government proposes to make some important changes to the entitlement provisions. It is the intention that interest will not be payable:

(a) for any year where the ratepayer only paid his rates after being summonsed, without seeking to defend his action in the magistrates' court. This is to address wilful default situations. Ratepayers who can persuade a billing authority to withdraw a summons on the grounds that the amount billed is not in fact payable, or who successfully defend non-payment in the magistrates' court, will not be denied interest on an overpayment;

(b) to the extent that overpayment merely arises from the way in which instalments are structured. This is primarily to avoid liability to interest just because a ratepayer moves out of a property during a year, rather than at the end of a year. (The instalment scheme is effectively front-loaded.)

Where interest is due, it is credited to the ratepayer as soon as practicable. However, if the alteration to the rating list falls to be made as a result of an order of a Valuation Tribunal or of the Lands Tribunal, the interest is not required to be credited before the expiry of thirty-five days from the date of the relevant order (reg 3(4) SI 1990 No 1904).

This is to allow for the possibility that the valuation officer may appeal against the decision of a tribunal. In such cases, he is required to notify the billing authority at the same time as he appeals or as soon as practicable after any such appeal or application for a review of a decision.

Although the billing authority must refund actual rates overpaid arising from the tribunal's decision, it is not required to pay interest on such refund if an appeal has been lodged. If the appellate tribunal determines a higher figure, the billing authority is entitled to recover the rates difference, but cannot recover interest paid. Accordingly, there is no requirement to pay interest if the decision of the lower body has been appealed against.

(b) Rate of interest

The interest rate to be applied in each financial year will be 1 per cent less than the bank base rate on the preceding 15 March (reg 4 SI 1991 No 2111).

Interest is payable on the assumption that the total overpayment for any year arises through that year. This is to reflect the staged instalments by which overpayments will generally accumulate.

However, the Government is now of the opinion that with the progressive reduction in base rates in recent years, a 1 per cent abatement now represents proportionately a much greater reduction than when the formula was first set. It is proposing that the amount of the deduction from the base rate should be tapered and banded to give a more consistent proportion of interest rates. The following table shows the suggested bands and reductions.

BASE RATE(%)		REDUCTION (%)
Exceeding	*Not exceeding*	
–	3.75	0.25
3.75	6.25	0.50
6.25	8.75	0.75
8.75	11.25	1.00
11.25	13.75	1.25
13.75	–	1.50

The following are examples which demonstrate some of the principles of the Regulations.

Example A

A hereditament was entered in the rating list at 1 April 1995 at a rateable value of £50,000. On 15 October 1995 the valuation officer altered the list reducing the assessment to £40,000 with an effective date of 1 April 1995. The billing authority calculated the adjustment on 22 November 1995. It is assumed that the ratepayer was liable for the non-domestic rates throughout the chargeable year and that rate liabilities were not subject to transitional limits. The uniform business rate for properties in England is 0.432 for the financial year 1995–1996.

By the time the list was altered the ratepayer had paid seven out of ten instalments.

Total rate liability: £50,000 × £0.432 = £21,600

Total amount paid by ratepayer: £2,160 × 7 = £15,120

$$\frac{£21,600}{10} = £2,160$$

Ratepayer's adjusted total liability for 1 April 1995 – 31 March 1996 is £40,000 × £0.432 = £17,280.

In this case the adjusted total liability for the chargeable year is £17,280, which is greater than the amount already paid by the ratepayer of £15,120, so in effect there is no overpayment in this case. As there are three instalments remaining, the balance of rates due of £2,160 can be paid by three instalments of £720.

Overpayment

An important point to realise when considering the question of overpayment is the fact that the use of the statutory instalment scheme has a 'front loading effect' with regard to the payments. Rates liability is calculated on a daily basis whereas rates payment is normally made by ten instalments. For example, assume rates due for the chargeable year are £12,000, giving a repayment of £1,200 (based on ten instalments), while the daily rate is:

$$\frac{£12,000}{365} = £32.87.$$

After two repayments the total paid by the ratepayer is £2,400; assuming sixty-one days had elapsed, the accrued liability is 61 × £32,87 = £2,005.07.

The definition of overpayment, which is contained in regulation 3(5) of SI 1991 No 2111, means that the amount paid in the relevant period towards the discharge of a ratepayers' liability, as established at the time of payment, exceeds his total liability as determined in consequence of the alteration of the rating list. It is therefore important to calculate not only the sums actually paid but also the sums which should have been paid disregarding the instalments scheme. Many ratepayers' bills will have been affected by the operation of the transitional arrangements. In these circumstances a reduction in the assessment may not result in a reduced rates bill and no interest will accordingly be due.

Relevant period

The definition of relevant period is contained in regulation 2(2) of SI 1990 No 1904; in simple terms the relevant period runs from 1 April of the chargeable financial year until the day before repayment day. This is assuming that the ratepayer was liable for the rates throughout the whole period. However, the Government intends to introduce new legislation to alter the relevant period to include the repayment day.

If the repayment day is 10 October 1995, the relevant period is from 1 April 1995 until 9 October 1995 (or 10 October if a change is made in the light of current government pronouncements).

Where the repayment of interest falls within the chargeable year in which the alteration to the rating list was made, and the ratepayer was liable throughout the relevant period, the following formula is used to calculate the interest to be repaid:

$$\frac{A \times B \times r}{2C \times 100}$$

where: A = the amount of the overpayment in relation to the relevant period;
B = the number of days in that period;
C = the number of days in the chargeable financial year;
r = the appropriate rate of interest expressed as a percentage.

The original definition of B was amended by SI 1991 No 2111 to correct an error in the principal Regulations, SI 1990 No 1904. This could have had the effect of overpayments of interest in cases where the alteration of a rating list took effect from a date after 1 April or the commencement of liability. For calculating interest for alterations between 1 April 1990 and 15 October 1990, reference should be made to the 1990 Regulations, but thereafter the definition of B in the 1991 Regulations should be used:

> B = the number of days in the relevant period or, where the effective date falls after the beginning of that period, the number of days in the period beginning on the effective date and ending on the last day of the relevant period.

It should be emphasised that interest will be paid at only half the appropriate rate to reflect the fact that the payments have been spread over a period of time under the statutory instalment scheme.

Example B

A hereditament had an entry in the rating list on 1 April 1990 at £85,000. The valuation officer agreed to an alteration in the rating list, thereby reducing the rateable value to £60,000; the valuation officer altered the list on 20 January 1991, with an effective date of 1 April 1990. The overpayment of rates was paid by the billing authority on 31 March 1991 (at the end of the chargeable year).

The relevant period runs from 1 April 1990 until 30 March 1991.

The ratepayer has paid the ten instalments amounting to a full liability of:

$$£85,000 \times £0.348 = £29,580$$

The adjusted liability due to the alteration of the rating list is:

$$£60,000 \times £0.348 = £20,880$$

The overpayment over the chargeable year was £8,700.

Interest is calculated as $\dfrac{A \times B \times r}{2C \times 100}$

$$\frac{8,700 \times 365 \times 14}{2 \times 365 \times 100} = £609$$

The gross interest repayment is £609.

Billing authorities are required to deduct tax on all interest payments at a rate of 25 per cent. The actual repayment will therefore be £456.75. They will also issue a certificate showing the tax deducted.

Subsequent period

It is important to distinguish between the relevant period and the subsequent period, since the interest calculations with regard to each are different.

A subsequent period is defined in regulation 2(2)(b): it begins with the day after the end of a relevant period and ends on the day immediately preceding the repayment day. Interest to be paid during this period is at the full rate, because the repayment will have been outstanding throughout this period.

The formula for determining the interest is as follows:

$$\frac{F \times G \times r}{c \times 100}$$

where: F = the amount of the overpayment in relation to the relevant period to which the subsequent period relates;

G = The number of days in the subsequent period;

c = the number of days in the year;

r = the rate of interest expressed as a percentage.

Example C

Use the facts given in Example B, but in this case assume the ratepayer sold the property and moved out on 30 November 1990.

The relevant period is from 1 April 1990 until 29 November 1990 (243 days). The subsequent period is from 30 November 1990 until 31 March 1991 (122 days).

Total liability for chargeable year:

$$£85,000 \times £0.348 = £29,580.$$

On the basis of ten instalments, the ratepayer had paid eight instalments of £2,958 each. Total paid = £23,664.

Adjusted liability following the alteration of the rating list over the relevant period:

$$\frac{£60,000 \times £0.348 \times 243}{365} = £13,900.93$$

The ratepayer's liability over the relevant period before adjustment of the rating list is:

$$\frac{£85,000 \times £0.348 \times 243}{365} = £19,692.98$$

The ratepayer has overpaid with regard to the relevant period:

$$£19,692.98 - £13,900.93 = £5,792.05$$

Interest on the overpayment for the relevant period is calculated as follows:

$$\frac{A \times B \times r}{2C \times 100}$$

$$\frac{£5,792.05 \times 243 \times 14}{2 \times 365 \times 100} = £269.92$$

Interest on the subsequent period (122 days) is calculated as:

$$\frac{F \times G \times r}{c \times 100}$$

$$\frac{£5,792.05 \times 122 \times 14}{365 \times 100} = £271.03$$

Total gross interest repayments is £269.92 + £271.03 = £540.95

However, the ratepayer has overpaid a total amount of £9,763.07 (i.e. £23,664 – £13,900.93). This full amount will be repaid to him plus the interest due. The interest was calculated on an overpayment of £5,792.05; the remaining repayment of £3,971.02 (i.e. £23,664 – £19,692.98) does not attract interest.

Example D

A property had a rateable value at 1 April 1990 of £270,000. This was reduced to £245,000 by the valuation officer on 10 November 1994 with a repayment date of 1 April 1995 and an effective date of 1 April 1990.

Year	Original liability £	Revised liability £	Refund £
1990/91	93,960	85,260	8,700
1991/92	104,220	94,570	9,650
1992/93	108,540	98,490	10,050
1993/94	112,320	101,920	10,400
1994/95	114,210	103,635	10,575

Interest rates: 1990/91 — 14%; 1991/92 — 12%; 1992/93 — 9.5%; 1993/94 — 5%; 1994/95 — 4.25%.

(a) 1990/91 Overpayment

(i) Relevant period   1/4/90–31/3/91

$$\frac{A \times B \times r}{2c \times 100} = \frac{8,700 \times 365 \times 14}{2 \times 365 \times 100}$$

$$= \quad \textbf{£609}$$

(ii)   Subsequent periods   1/4/91–31/3/92

$$\frac{F \times G \times r}{c \times 100} = \frac{8{,}700 \times 365 \times 12}{365 \times 100}$$

$$= \textbf{£1,044}$$

1/4/92–31/3/93

$$\frac{8{,}700 \times 365 \times 9.5}{365 \times 100}$$

$$= \textbf{£826.50}$$

1/4/93–31/3/94

$$\frac{8{,}700 \times 365 \times 5}{365 \times 100}$$

$$= \textbf{£435}$$

1/4/94–31/3/95

$$\frac{8{,}700 \times 365 \times 4.25}{365 \times 100}$$

$$= \textbf{£369.75}$$

(b) 1991/92 Overpayment

(i)   Relevant period   1/4/91–31/3/92

$$\frac{A \times B \times r}{2 \times c \times 100} = \frac{9{,}650 \times 365 \times 12}{2 \times 365 \times 100}$$

$$= \textbf{£579}$$

(ii)   Subsequent periods   1/4/92–31/3/93

$$\frac{9{,}650 \times 365 \times 9.5}{365 \times 100}$$

$$= \textbf{£916.75}$$

1/4/93–31/3/94

$$\frac{9{,}650 \times 365 \times 5}{365 \times 100}$$

$$= \textbf{£482.50}$$

$$1/4/94-31/3/95$$

$$\frac{9,650 \times 365 \times 4.25}{365 \times 100}$$

$$= \quad \textbf{£410.12}$$

(c) 1992/93 Overpayment

(i) Relevant period   1/4/92–31/3/93

$$\frac{10,050 \times 365 \times 9.5}{2 \times 365 \times 100}$$

$$= \quad \textbf{£477.37}$$

(ii) Subsequent periods   1/4/93–31/3/94

$$\frac{10,050 \times 365 \times 5}{365 \times 100}$$

$$= \quad \textbf{£502.50}$$

$$1/4/94-31/3/95$$

$$\frac{10,050 \times 365 \times 4.25}{365 \times 100}$$

$$= \quad \textbf{£427.12}$$

(d) 1993/94 Overpayment

(i) Relevant period   14/4/93–31/3/94

$$\frac{10,400 \times 365 \times 5}{2 \times 100 \times 365}$$

$$= \quad \textbf{£260}$$

(ii) Subsequent periods   1/4/94–31/3/95

$$\frac{10,400 \times 365 \times 4.25}{365 \times 100}$$

$$= \quad \textbf{£442}$$

(e) 1994/95 Overpayment

(i) Relevant period   1/4/94–31/3/95

$$\frac{10{,}575 \times 365 \times 4.25}{2 \times 365 \times 100}$$

=   **£224.71**

Total interest (gross)	£8,006.32
tax @ 25%	£2,001.58
net of tax refund	£6,004.74

A quicker alternative approach would be as follows:

Year	Refund £		Factor		Interest £
1990/91	8,700	×	0.3775	=	3,284.24
1991/92	9,650	×	0.2475	=	2,388.37
1992/93	10,050	×	0.14	=	1,407.00
1993/94	10,400	×	0.0675	=	702.00
1994/95	10,575	×	0.02125	=	224.71

£8,006.32 gross interest

The above multiplication factors have been calculated as follows:

For overpayments for 1990/91

1990/91	14% ÷ 2	=	0.07
1991/92		=	0.12
1992/93		=	0.095
1993/94		=	0.05
1994/95		=	0.0425
		=	0.3775

For overpayments for 1991/92

1991/92	12% ÷ 2	=	0.06
1992/93		=	0.095
1993/94		=	0.05
1994/95		=	0.0425
		=	0.2475

and so on.

It must be emphasised that where a ratepayer pays irregular amounts in different years, before an assessment is reduced, then this could materially affect his interest calculations, even if no formal action is taken by the billing authority, since there could be some years where he has not overpaid and subsequent ones where the amount of overpayment is greater because of earlier deficits.

Chapter 3

Valuation Tribunals and the Lands Tribunal

A. Valuation Tribunals

Relevant legislation:

- Schedule 11 to the Local Government Finance Act 1988;
- Valuation and Community Charge Tribunals Regulations 1989 (SI 1989 No 439);
- Valuation and Community Charge Tribunals (Transfer of Jurisdiction) Regulations 1989 (SI 1989 No 440);
- Non-Domestic Rating (Alteration of Lists and Appeals) Regulations 1993 (SI 1993 No 291);
- Valuation and Community Charge Tribunals (Amendment) Regulations 1993 (SI 1993 No 292);
- Valuation and Community Charge Tribunals (Amendment) (England) Regulations 1995 (SI 1995 No 363).

1. Introduction

During the period from 1862 until 1948, the tribunal responsible for hearing disputed assessments was the local assessment committee. The Local Government Act 1948 absolished assessment committees and in their place provided for the establishment of local valuation courts. These courts were given wider powers than the assessment committees; for example they could require evidence to be given on oath. Since 1948, local valuation courts have been the forum for the hearing of rating appeals. However, with the passing of LGFA 1988, the local valuation courts were replaced by the Valuation and Community Charge Tribunals ('VCCTs'). The change of name reflected the tribunal's new role of hearing appeals against the community charge. However, with the repeal of the community charge and the introduction of the council tax, section 15 of the LGFA 1992 provides that the VCCTs should now be known as Valuation Tribunals with responsibility for council tax appeals.

By virtue of section 136 and Schedule 11 to the LGFA 1988, regulations governing the establishment and powers of the Valuation Tribunal are contained in SI 1989 No 439.

The Valuation Tribunal is an independent body established under the LGFA 1988, with detailed provisions regarding appointment of members, duration of membership, disqualification from membership, appointment of the president and chairman of the tribunal included in the Valuation and Community Charge Tribunals Regulations 1989 (SI 1989 No 439).

It was one of the strengths of the local valuation courts that people could attend and present their case without professional representation and in a simple and informal manner; it remains the Government's intention that the Valuation Tribunals should operate in a similar manner, this intention being expressed in regulation 28(13) of the Non-Domestic Rating (Alteration of Lists and Appeals) Regulations (repealed) (SI 1990 No 582), which declares that the tribunal should '... seek to avoid formality in its proceedings'. (See also reg 40 Non-Domestic Rating (Alteration of Lists and Appeals) Regulations (SI 1993 No 291).)

The Transfer of Jurisdiction Regulations (SI 1989 No 440) came into force on 1 May 1989, and from that date the jurisdiction conferred on the local valuation courts by various statutes, e.g. the General Rate Act 1967 and the Rating (Disabled Persons) Act 1978, was transferred to the VCCTs and their successor. The General Rate Act 1967 continues to be applicable on and after 1 April 1990 in respect of appeals relating to the 1973 valuation list.

2. Role of the Valuation Tribunal

The jurisdiction of the Valuation Tribunal falls under the following categories:

(a) Valuation

Appeals on matters relating to questions of valuation, that is, the determination of the correct rateable value. In addition, the tribunal has the power to determine the appropriate effective date of the alteration. Previously on this matter recourse was to the magistrates' court. Furthermore, the tribunal can now determine issues relating to exemptions and whether a property is domestic or not.

(b) Validity

A proposal which has been made but the valuation officer considers it to be invalid by virtue of regulation 7(1) of SI 1993 No 291. Unless the invalidity notice is withdrawn, the maker of the proposal can within four weeks of the service of the invalidity notice appeal against the notice to the Valuation Tribunal, or indeed make a further proposal unless the initial proposal was out of time.

Issues pertaining to invalidity prior to the above-mentioned regulations would have had to be determined by judicial review, which in many cases can be an expensive way to resolve the problem.

The Valuation Tribunal will not hear an appeal under regulation 12 (SI 1993 No 291) until any appeal under regulation 7 in respect of the same proposal has been determined (reg 33(2) SI 1993 No 291).

With regard to the central rating list, the Valuation Tribunal has the power to determine disagreements as to whether a proposal is well founded.

(c) Completion notices

An appeal against a completion notice must be made within four weeks of the date of service of the notice (reg 29 SI 1993 No 291). Before the hearing, the matter can still be agreed by the respective parties.

(d) Certification

A certification of value by the valuation officer (reg 30 SI 1993 No 291 and reg 36 Non-Domestic Rating (Chargeable Amounts) Regulations 1994 (SI 1994 No 3279)). Such certificates of value can also apply to transitional arrangements. Where an interested person is dissatisfied with the value certified, he may serve notice on the valuation officer within six months of the date of issue of the certificate. If the notice is not withdrawn (within four weeks of service) or there is no written agreement within four weeks of the date of service of the notice, between the valuation officer and the appellant on the value which should be certified, the matter is referred to the Valuation Tribunal.

It is the duty of the president of the Valuation Tribunal to secure the arrangements for the hearing of appeals. The tribunal will not consider the substantive merits of a proposal while there is still an outstanding appeal regarding the validity of the proposal.

Where there are two or more appeals affecting the same hereditament, the Valuation Tribunal will deal with them in the order in which the alterations proposed would take effect (reg 33(3) SI 1993 No 291).

3. Withdrawals

Proposals may be withdrawn at any time before the hearing of a relevant appeal by the Valuation Tribunal or before consideration of the written representations. Notice of the withdrawal must be given to the clerk of the tribunal:

(a) in the case of an appeal against a competition notice, by the appellant in writing; and

(b) in any other case, by the valuation officer.

It is incumbent upon the valuation officer to obtain the written consent of all parties to the appeal for the withdrawal of the appeal.

If the valuation officer alters the list in accordance with the proposal, or written agreement is reached between the parties to an appeal, the appeal is deemed to have been withdrawn when the valuation officer notifies the clerk to the tribunal.

4. Written representations

Under regulation 35 of SI 1993 No 291, provided that all parties agree, an appeal may be disposed of on the basis of written representations. Once such an agreement has been reached, the clerk will advise all the parties accordingly; within four weeks of such a notice, each party may serve on the clerk a notice stating:

(a) his reasons or further reasons in support of his contentions; or

(b) that he does not wish to make further representations.

The clerk will then serve copies of the above on all the other parties who then have a further four weeks in which to reply formally to the other party's representations, and copies of any such further notices are also served by the clerk on all the other parties.

At the end of another four-week period, the matter is referred to a tribunal; such referral comprises copies of all the notices and the original information under regulation 35(5).

At that point the tribunal may:

(a) require any party to furnish further written details of the grounds of appeal and any other relevant facts; or

(b) order that the appeal be disposed of by hearing.

Previously, under the provisions for written representations it was provided that the Valuation Tribunal could require a party to attend in order to give evidence, and also the other parties to the proceedings could attend if they so wished. This approach created a 'hearing' situation in the context of a disposal of the appeal by written representations. The 1993 Regulations (SI 1993 No 291) have withdrawn this power (reg 35(6)).

Written representations are expected to provide a moderately quick and effective procedure for resolving fairly straightforward appeals, such as disputes over the issue of a completion notice or the validity of a proposal.

5. Pre-hearing review

Either on the written application of a party or on the decision of the chairman, a pre-hearing review can be held in order to determine the extent to which the facts can be agreed or to clarify the issues to be dealt with at a hearing (reg 36). This procedure can prove useful in respect of the more complex cases, and it may avoid the need to postpone a hearing where one party has not been made aware of, or is not in possession of, evidence presented by another.

6. Notice of hearing

Where an appeal is to be determined at a hearing, the clerk to the tribunal will give each party at least four weeks' notice of the date, time and place of the hearing (reg 37 SI 1993 No 291).

7. Representation

All parties to a hearing may appear in person, or with assistance from counsel, a solicitor or other representative (provided that that person is not a member, clerk or other employee of the relevant Valuation Tribunal).

The Valuation Tribunal cannot award costs, which means that the parties will each have to meet their respective costs in preparing and presenting their case.

8. Conduct of hearing

The Valuation Tribunal generally consists of a chairman and two members. In exceptional circumstances, and where all parties agree, the tribunal may comprise only two members. The hearing is held in public, unless a party applies for a private hearing and convinces the tribunal that it would be prejudicial to their interests for the hearing to be held in public. If all parties to an appeal, with the exception of the valuation officer, fail to appear, the Valuation Tribunal has the power to dismiss the appeal (reg 40(4)), or in other circumstances to determine the appeal in the absence of the party.

The Valuation Tribunal has the power to require evidence to be given by oath or affirmation.

In the case of a valuation officer's alteration of a local list, or his refusal to process a proposal on the ground that it is invalid, the valuation officer begins the hearing. In respect of an appeal against a completion notice, the billing authority begins the hearing. Subsequently, the tribunal hears parties as it thinks fit. Parties are entitled to call witnesses who may be subject to cross-examination.

The tribunal has a wide discretion as to how a particular hearing should be conducted, and is specifically required by the regulations to seek to avoid formality in its proceedings. Furthermore it is not bound by any enactments or rules of law relating to the admissibility of evidence.

The hearing of appeals may be postponed (reg 37(4)) in advance of the hearing. The tribunal can adjourn appeals for such time and on such terms as the tribunal thinks fit. A reasonable notice of the time and place to which the hearing has been adjourned shall be given to each party to the proceedings.

A tribunal, after giving notice to the parties inviting them to be present, may inspect any appeal hereditament. This does not include an inspection of the comparables submitted in evidence. However, if the parties wish this to be done they must make the necessary arrangements.

9. Evidence

Information to be used as evidence is governed by regulation 41 of SI 1993 No 291. The regulation deals with information to be supplied by billing authorities and those cases where the valuation officer serves a notice on a person requiring him to supply information. Information obtained from rent returns under section 82 of the General Rate Act 1967 may be admissible as evidence in appeal proceedings, as is information contained in returns made under Schedule 9(5) paragraphs (1)–(4) to the LGFA 1988. This provides that the valuation officer give not less than two weeks' notice specifying that information and allows any party to the proceedings to inspect and copy the relevant records on 24 hours' notice. Where the valuation officer implements this procedure, the other party may before the hearing serve on the valuation officer a notice specifying other comparable hereditaments to be used and requiring the valuation officer to allow inspection and copying of any document containing information which is in the possession of the valuation officer. The valuation officer is obliged to produce at the hearing all the relevant documents.

Under this procedure the number of comparable hereditaments should not exceed four. However, the regulations provide that the party to the appeal may serve notice on the valuation officer specifying the same number of hereditaments as are being used by the valuation officer.

The documentary evidence to be supplied by the valuation officer should only contain information in relation to direct evidence of the rent payable, and any other information which is reasonably required for the purposes of the appeal. The main purpose of this is to protect commercially sensitive information such as 'barrelage' in the case of public houses.

Regulation 41(7) of SI 1993 No 291 allows an application to be made to the tribunal where the valuation officer refuses to comply with the notice.

10. Decisions

The appeal is decided by a majority of members. Where the tribunal comprises two members, and they are unable to agree, the appeal is remitted for determination by way of a fresh hearing with three different members. The tribunal is under an obligation to notify the parties in writing of its decision, and must give reasons for its decision. A decision of the Valuation Tribunal may be reserved or given orally at the end of the hearing. As soon as reasonably practicable thereafter, the decision or confirmation of the oral decision must be notified in writing to the parties, with a statement of reasons for it (reg 43 SI 1993 No 291).

Following its decision with regard to appeals under regulations 12, 28 and 30 of SI 1993 No 291, the Valuation Tribunal may by order direct the valuation officer to:

(a) alter the rating list in accordance with its decision; or
(b) alter any determination or certificate issued in respect of the transitional arrangements.

The valuation officer is obliged to comply with the order within six weeks of its being made. This has been reduced to two weeks for orders concerning the 1995 rating lists (reg 21 Non-Domestic Rating (Alteration of Lists and Appeals) Regulations (SI 1995 No 609)).

Regulation 44 of SI 1993 No 291 has given Valuation Tribunals the power to determine a disputed rateable value at a figure greater than either that sought in the originating proposal or shown in the list. In such an event, however, the effective date of the alteration is the date of the Valuation Tribunal's decision and not the date of the originating proposal. The scope of this regulation is a radical departure from the limits under the old system (under the General Rate Act 1967) where the 'alteration proposed' and the 'figure appearing in the list' set the boundaries of the court's powers, save in a few exceptional cases. The introduction of such an open-ended risk may well concentrate appellants' minds before an actual hearing. By virtue of regulation 47(5), such a power is also available on the hearing of any further appeal by the Lands Tribunal.

This power clearly indicates the importance of the local knowledge of the members and chairman of the Valuation Tribunal. However, if neither the appellant nor the valuation officer gives evidence in support of an assessment higher than that appearing in the list, it is difficult to envisage circumstances in which the local tribunal could properly arrive at such a decision. Since a valuation officer may alter a rating list at any time, if on the hearing of an appeal seeking a reduced assessment he endeavours to advocate a figure higher than that already in the list, the tribunal may give little weight to this part of his evidence, as he is effectively impugning his own list.

In view of the above, it may be wondered why such a power was introduced. It should be borne in mind, however, that the powers given to the Lands Tribunal can only be the same as those available to the Valuation Tribunals. It is thought likely that this regulation was introduced more to widen the ability of the Lands Tribunal to determine assessments in an unfettered way, without the need for cross-appeals, rather than to give Valuation Tribunals an unlimited power with which to frighten appellants.

Review of decisions

Under the General Rate Act 1967 a local valuation court could set aside its decisions where statutory requirements were not met. The new system allows Valuation Tribunals to set aside or review their decisions. The Valuation Tribunal may dismiss an application for a review where it is not made within four weeks from the date when the decision was notified in writing to the parties (reg 45(3)).

Any person who was a party to an appeal and who is aggrieved by the decision of the Valuation Tribunal may apply in writing to the clerk of the tribunal giving reasons for the tribunal to review, or set aside that decision. In respect of an appeal relating to the validity of a proposal, the contents of a rating list, or a valuation officer's certificate, the grounds for such a review are:

(i) that the decision was wrongly made as a result of a clerical error;

(ii) that a party did not appear, and can show reasonable cause why he did not do so;

(iii) that the decision is affected by a decision of, or an appeal from, the High Court or Lands Tribunal in relation to an appeal in respect of the same hereditament which was the subject of the tribunal's decision;

(iv) where the appeal related to a completion notice a further ground can apply: that new evidence which could not have been foreseen has become available since the hearing.

Where the tribunal sets aside its previous decision it must revoke any order made as a consequence of that decision and order a rehearing or redetermination before the same or different tribunal.

11. Further appeal

Regulation 47 of SI 1993 No 291 provides a right to a further appeal to the Lands Tribunal against a Valuation Tribunal's decision in respect of appeals relating to the validity of proposals, the proposed alteration of local and central rating lists, certifications and completion notices. The right of appeal to the Lands Tribunal is limited to those parties who appeared at the Valuation Tribunal hearing or, if the appeal was disposed of by written representations, who made such representations.

Appeals to the Lands Tribunal should be initiated within four weeks of the decision or order of the Valuation Tribunal – otherwise they may be dismissed. However, regulation 47(2)(b) appears to open the door for an appeal to the Lands Tribunal against the original decision (reg 47(1)) where parties did not appear and whose application under regulation 45 has not been successful.

12. Arbitration

If, before the Valuation Tribunal hearing or consideration of written representations, all the parties agree in writing, the matter can be referred to arbitration. In this case section 31 of the Arbitration Act

1950 applies to the proceedings. The arbitrator has the same powers as those given to the Valuation Tribunal as regards the making of any order (reg 48 SI 1993 No 291).

13. Notification of further proceedings

Where the valuation officer applies to a tribunal for a review of a decision in consequence of which an order requiring the alteration of a rating list was made, or appeals to the Lands Tribunal, he must at the same time, or as soon as is reasonably practicable thereafter, notify the relevant billing authority or the appropriate Secretary of State in respect of central list appeals. He must also notify the clerk of the tribunal of any relevant appeals to the Lands Tribunal, and a billing authority has a similar responsibility in respect of completion notice appeals.

B. The Lands Tribunal

1. History of the Lands Tribunal

Before the establishment of the Lands Tribunal, matters which form the substantive elements of its work today were dealt with by a number of other bodies. Compensation disputes were considered by official arbitrators appointed under the Acquisition of Land (Assessment of Compensation) Act 1919, estate duty matters were dealt with by a panel of referees appointed under the Finance (1909–1910) Act 1910, and rating appeals were determined by the Quarter Sessions.

The Lands Tribunal was established by the Lands Tribunal Act 1949, and formally came into existence on 1 June 1950. Its status is equivalent to that of the High Court. The tribunal comprises a President, being a person who has held judicial office or who is a barrister of at least seven years' standing, supported by members who are barristers or solicitors similarly qualified together with surveyor members appointed after consultation with the President of the Royal Institution of Chartered Surveyors.

2. Disposal without a hearing

An appeal may be withdrawn by sending to the Registrar a written notice of withdrawal signed by all the parties. Such a withdrawal can therefore only be made with the agreement of the other side which may include conditions and/or payment of costs.

An appellant has the opportunity at any time before the commencement of the hearing to apply to the President for an order to strike out or dismiss the appeal. The President if he feels it appropriate may grant such an order.

Where the parties agree that the appeal should be settled by consent, upon such agreed terms, the appropriate course of action is to submit the terms of agreement to the tribunal, signed by all parties, and an order is then made by the tribunal in accordance with the agreed terms.

In those cases which are considered to be 'simple' or relatively straightforward the matter may be dealt with by written representations (rule 33A). This procedure tends to be infrequently used, with the tribunal preferring to hold an oral hearing whenever it is reasonable to do so.

3. Pre-trial reviews

This particular approach is now becoming more popular, its objectives being to expedite matters, to have simple hearings and to keep costs reasonable. A member of the tribunal or the registrar may decide to hold a pre-trial review, or any party to the appeal may apply for one. The review should ideally enable the parties to agree as many of the facts as possible and to identify the issues to be more formally considered at the hearing.

4. Appearances

An appeal against the decision of a Valuation Tribunal may be made within four weeks from the date of decision, by the sending to the registrar of the Lands Tribunal a notice of appeal in writing, indicating an intention to appeal. The appellant should send with his notice of appeal copies of the notice to be served upon the valuation officer and a list of all other persons who appeared before the Valuation Tribunal. He should also send a copy of the decision of the Valuation Tribunal and a copy of the rating proposal or determination which was the subject of the proceedings of the Valuation Tribunal.

Persons who appeared before the Valuation Tribunal and are aggrieved by its decision have the right to appeal to the Lands Tribunal. Those who have the right to appear before the Lands Tribunal include the valuation officer, an interested party (as defined in reg 2 SI 1993 No 291) which includes the occupier, and the billing authority in certain circumstances (s 144 LGFA 1988).

5. Appeal procedure

When a notice of appeal from the decision of the Valuation Tribunal is lodged with the Lands Tribunal, a copy is served on all those who appeared as a party to the proceedings at the Valuation Tribunal. Every person on whom a copy of a notice of appeal has been served must indicate if he intends to appear at the hearing and to give notice of this intention to the registrar and to the appellant, such notice often being referred to as a 'noita'.

Where an appeal is on a point of law, or the rateable value of the hereditament to which the appeal relates exceeds £1,250, then the appellant must serve pleadings. The general rule is that the appellant must send to the registrar and to each party intending to appear a statement of his case. This Statement of Case may include the following:

- the history of the appeal;
- details of the parties to the appeal;
- the facts to be proved;
- points of law at issue;
- summary of the appellant's contentions.

The respondent is in turn required within twenty-eight days of receiving the Statement of Case to send a Reply to the registrar for passing to the appellant. This document must set out details on the facts to be proved and any points of law on which the respondent intends to rely. Normally, the Reply:

- includes those aspects of the appellant's case which can be agreed;
- sets out those points which are challenged;
- lists any further facts;
- summarises the respondent's contentions.

In those cases where the dispute involves matters of valuation, all parties are required to submit their valuations and details of the comparables they intend to rely on. These additional documents are submitted at the same time as the appellant lodges his Statement of Case and the respondent his Reply.

6. Hearing

The hearing before the Lands Tribunal is not a rehearing of the case, but a *de novo* hearing. This means that the parties are not bound by the arguments presented before the earlier Valuation Tribunal. However, arguments and valuations used at the Valuation

Tribunal may be relevant and one would expect consistency of approach between the two forums.

The tribunal normally sits in public unless it is dealing with:

- a rule 33A case, i.e. by written representations;
- a settlement of questions for a case stated;
- a case in which national security is involved.

The hearing is complete in itself and the decision is made on the evidence submitted at the hearing. Generally the appellant makes an opening statement, covering the history of the appeal, the pleadings, any statement of agreed facts, his own (or other parties') legal authorities followed by the calling of his expert witnesses. After all the appellant's expert witnesses have been cross-examined by the respondent it is the turn of the respondent to present his case and to have his expert witnesses cross-examined by the appellant. At the conclusion of all the evidence the parties may make closing statements in the reverse order from that in which they gave evidence, so the appellant has the last word.

7. Expert evidence

The Lands Tribunal Rules provide that normally each party will be limited to one expert witness, but this can be extended in complex cases. The proceedings in the Lands Tribunal are governed in accordance with the rules of evidence. Evidence is given on oath and subject to cross-examination in the normal course of events. Evidence before the tribunal must be given orally or, if the parties consent or the President so orders, by affidavit. However, the tribunal can at any stage make an order requiring the personal attendance of any party for examination and cross-examination.

In appeals concerning questions of value it is unlikely that evidence would be accepted in affidavit form. If a question of value is the principal issue it is important that the expert witnesses can be cross-examined on their evidence. One of the problems, concerning evidence relates to the admissibility of evidence and the fact that hearsay is inadmissible. In *Subramaniam v Public Prosecutor* [1956] 1 WLR 965 hearsay was explained by the Privy Council as follows:

'Evidence of a statement made to a witness by a person who is not himself called as a witness may or may not be hearsay. It is hearsay and inadmissible when the object of the evidence is to establish the truth of what is contained in the statement. It is not hearsay and is admissible when it is proposed to establish by the evidence, not the truth of the statement but the fact that it was made.'

Questions often arise as to what extent the expert's opinions of value are founded on direct personal experience and how far they are based on what he has been told by others. It is important to realise that the opinion evidence of the expert witness is based on his own experience. Megarry J in *English Exporters v Eldonwall Ltd* [1973] 1 Ch 415 had this to say on the position of the expert witness:

'As an expert witness, the valuer is entitled to express his opinion about matters within his field of competence. In building up his opinions about values, he will no doubt have learned much from transactions in which he has himself been engaged, and of which he could give first hand evidence. But he will also have learned much from many other sources, including much of which he could give no first hand evidence. Textbooks, journals, reports of auctions and other dealings, and information obtained from his professional brethren and others, some related to particular transactions and some more general and indefinite, will all have contributed their share .... Nevertheless, the opinion that the expert expresses is none the worse because it is in part derived from the matters of which he could give no direct evidence.'

An individual always has the right to present his own case before the tribunal. However, the parties are usually represented by counsel or solicitors or (by leave of the tribunal) by any other person. Valuers will not normally be given leave of the tribunal because of the difficulty of combining the dual roles of advocate and expert witness. The primary duty of an expert witness is to assist the tribunal by honest opinion on the matter in dispute, whereas an advocate's role is to advance arguments and commentary on the law.

8. Costs

On an appeal to the Lands Tribunal, the costs normally follow the event, i.e. the unsuccessful party is obliged to meet the costs of the successful party. However, it should be noted that costs remain at the discretion of the tribunal.

Where a ratepayer is unrepresented and unsuccessful in his appeal, the valuation officer will normally ask for costs, which are quantified and awarded against the ratepayer. Where the ratepayer has legal representation, the costs are based on either county court scales of costs or on the High Court scale depending on the complexity of the issues involved. When the parties are unable to agree the costs, the matter is referred back to the registrar of the tribunal to be taxed on the appropriate scale.

9. Decisions

The decision of the tribunal is given in writing together with the reasons for the decision. At the discretion of the tribunal the decision may be given orally provided that there would be no injustice to the parties. However, a written decision is more usual.

Decisions can take the form of a determination of value. The Lands Tribunal may confirm, vary, set aside, revoke or remit the decision of the Valuation Tribunal, and may make any order which the Valuation Tribunal could have made.

Decisions of the tribunal are not binding precedents although they are of significant persuasive value. The tribunal is the final arbiter or forum on matters relating to fact and valuation. An appeal by way of case stated, on a point of law only, lies with the Court of Appeal.

Chapter 4

Rating of unoccupied property

Historically the principle in rating has been to tax the occupier of property or land. This has been the case since 1601 with the passing of the Poor Relief Act. The principle continued without change until the introduction of unoccupied rating in section 21 of the Local Government Act 1966. As Lawton LJ pointed out in *Hastings Borough Council v Tarmac Properties Ltd* [1985] RA 124, the time came when Parliament wished to enable rating authorities to levy rates in respect of unoccupied property, the aim being to prevent owners from keeping property vacant to suit their own personal advantage, thereby depriving the rating authority of rates income.

The consolidating legislation, the General Rate Act 1967, contained the relevant provisions in section 17 and Schedule 1 (as amended by section 15 of the Local Government Act 1974). With the repeal of the 1967 Act, the statutory provisions relating to rating of unoccupied property are now contained in several pieces of legislation.

Relevant legislation:

- Sections 45, 46, 46A of and Schedule 4A to the Local Government Finance Act 1988;
- Non-Domestic Rating (Unoccupied Property) Regulations 1989 (SI 1989 No 2261);
- Schedule 5 to the Local Government and Housing Act 1989;
- Non-Domestic Rating (Unoccupied Property) (Amendment) Regulations 1995 (SI 1995 No 549).

Before 1990, rating authorities' power to levy the 'empty rate' was discretionary. Authorities could apply the rate in a flexible manner – the proportion of the full rate could range from 0 to 100 per cent. Rating authorities had the power to discriminate between different classes of property and could apply different rates to each.

The position has radically altered since 1 April 1990. No longer do billing authorities (previously rating and charging authorities) have the power to levy the empty rate. Power now lies with the

Secretary of State, who also sets the percentage applicable. At present the rating of unoccupied property is at a mandatory rate of 50 per cent of the occupied property rate. In effect, all unoccupied properties (excluding exempt property) are liable to pay empty rate based on 50 per cent of the full rate charge.

Gone are the days when authorities could introduce a degree of flexibility with regard to the type of property liable to unoccupied property rate. In the Government publication *Paying for Local Government* (July 1987), it was stated that only 40 per cent of local authorities actually exercised their discretion to levy unoccupied property rates. It is possible that the change to a mandatory rate of 50 per cent applied uniformly across England and Wales may lead to long-term problems in the supply of new buildings through its effect on developers.

There has been considerable debate on the fairness and equitable nature of the present mandatory system. It has been suggested that, in order to mitigate the effects of the unoccupied rate, the rate-free period should be extended from three months to twelve. A further possibility is to reduce the level of unoccupied rate from the existing 50 per cent to 10 per cent, a measure supported by the Royal Institution of Chartered Surveyors. It has even been argued that full exemption should be given to all vacant commercial property, a suggestion that is unlikely to gain government support, due principally to the potential loss of revenue. At the time of writing, revenue raised from the unoccupied rate was in excess of £575 million annually.

1. Liability

Before a hereditament becomes subject to a non-domestic rate, a number of conditions must be fulfilled (s 45(1) LGFA 1988):

(a) on the day none of the hereditament is occupied;

(b) on the day the ratepayer is the owner of the whole hereditament;

(c) the hereditament is shown for the day in the local rating list;

(d) on the day the hereditament falls within a class prescribed by the Secretary of State. A class may be prescribed by reference to a number of factors including the physical characteristics of hereditaments, the unoccupancy of hereditaments and the fact that owners of hereditaments fall within prescribed descriptions. By virtue of SI 1989 No 2261, the class of non-domestic hereditament prescribed for the purposes of section 45 consists of all 'relevant non-domestic hereditaments', with twelve exceptions (see pages 57–62).

Where a property is unoccupied, the owner is responsible for the payment of unoccupied property rates. 'Owner' is defined as the person entitled to possession of the hereditament (s 65(1) LGFA 1988).

The question of liability for non-domestic rates arose in *Kingston upon Thames Royal London Borough Council v Marlow* [1995] EGCS 161. In this case a dispute arose between the landlord and the tenant regarding the cost of repairs, with the landlord seeking forfeiture. The tenant then vacated the property, writing to the landlord that he was relinquishing the tenancy and returning the key. The landlord argued that, as the tenant's lease was unexpired, the tenant should be responsible for the rates. It was held by the High Court that, because the tenant had vacated the premises and the landlord had accepted termination of the lease, the landlord as the person in possession was liable for the non-domestic rates. The lesson for landlords in this situation is straightforward: if the tenant's covenants for liability for rent and rates (as occupier) are worth more than having the vacant possession of the premises, forfeiture of the lease should not be sought.

It should be noted that a building society under the powers conferred by section 7 of the Building Societies Act 1962 can hold land or buildings in connection with its business. A society, in its capacity as a mortgagee in possession, appears to have power under sections 99 and 101 of the Law of Property Act 1925 to sell and lease the property. It therefore falls within the definition of owner under section 65 of the LGFA 1988 and consequently can be liable to pay the unoccupied property rate.

2. Exemption

Before an unoccupied property is liable to be rated, it must be a relevant hereditament. In *Watford Borough Council v Parcourt Property Investment Company Ltd* [1971] RA 97, a recently built office block which was totally devoid of internal partitioning was held not to be a hereditament. But if a completion notice in respect of such a hereditament has been accepted, agreed or determined, the circumstances deemed under that notice would supplement the actual situation.

The Non-Domestic Rating (Unoccupied Property) Regulations 1989 (SI 1989 No 2261) provide for exemption of broadly the same hereditaments as were exempt under paragraph 2 of Schedule 1 to the General Rate Act 1967.

All classes of non-domestic hereditaments consisting of, or any part of, any building, together with any land ordinarily used or intended for use for the purposes of the building, are liable to unoccupied property rates *unless* the hereditament is prescribed by the Secretary of State as being exempt.

The categories of exemption apply to all 'relevant non-domestic hereditaments'. The definition of relevant non-domestic hereditament is to be found in section 64(4) of the LGFA 1988 and includes property of any of the following descriptions:

- lands;
- coal mines;
- mines of any other description, other than a mine of which royalties or dues are wholly reserved in kind;
- sporting rights (i.e. rights of fowling, shooting, fishing) when severed from the occupation of the land on which the rights are exercisable;
- land used for exhibiting advertisements.

It is interesting to note that under the previous legislation sporting rights and land used for exhibiting advertisements were deemed not to be a relevant hereditament, and consequently when unoccupied were not rateable. The law has now been amended so that such land, when unoccupied, is liable for unoccupied property rates.

Exempt categories

(a) Properties unoccupied for a continuous period not exceeding three months.

Properties unoccupied for a period not exceeding three months are entitled to full rate relief during that period. If the property remains unoccupied beyond the three month 'free period', the owner/ratepayer will be liable for unoccupied property rates. For the purpose of determining whether a property has been continuously unoccupied for three months, any period of occupation of less than six weeks is disregarded. This avoids the claiming of consecutive periods of rate relief after short terms of occupancy.

Where a building comprising a single hereditament has been unoccupied for more than three months and a new hereditament has been created (without structural alterations) which comprises part of the original hereditament, it seems that unoccupied property rates are recoverable on the new hereditament from the moment of its creation: *Brent London Borough Council v Ladbroke Rentals Ltd* [1981] RA 155.

If during the unoccupied period a change in ownership takes place, this makes no difference to the rate-free period, and therefore the new owner does not acquire the benefit of an additional rate-free period; see *Brent London Borough Council v Ladbroke Rentals Ltd*. Once the rate-free period has ended, the unoccupied property rate can be levied on the person entitled to possession of the hereditament: *Camden London Borough Council v Bromley Park Gardens Estates Ltd* [1985] 2 EGLR 179.

(b)   The owner is prohibited by law from occupying the hereditament or from allowing it to be occupied.

The circumstances falling within this category include statutory orders specifically precluding occupation, namely:

(i)   closing orders under section 267(2) of the Housing Act 1985;

(ii)   demolition orders under section 267(1) of the Housing Act 1985;

(iii) discontinuation orders under section 102 of the Town and Country Planning Act 1990 or section 13 of the Planning and Land Compensation Act 1992.

In the Court of Appeal case, *Regent Lion Properties Ltd v Westminster City Council* [1990] RA 121, it was claimed that the hereditament should be exempt from unoccupied rates on two grounds: (i) on the ground that occupation was prohibited by law following the service of a notice under the Health and Safety at Work Act 1974, which required remedial works to be carried out as brown asbestos was present; and (ii) because a time-limited planning permission under which the property had been occupied had expired, and for that reason the company was prohibited by law from occupying the hereditament.

In relation to the first ground, Glidewell LJ said the notice under the 1974 Act 'had the inevitable effect of preventing rateable occupation until both the remedial work to cure the asbestos problem and the subsequent refurbishment work had been carried out. Since that was the inevitable effect, in my judgement the effect of the notice was to prohibit by law the occupation of the premises until the remedial work had been completed'.

On the second ground Glidewell LJ said:

> 'In my judgement, the law does not prohibit an owner or occupier of property from using it for a particular purpose simply because planning permission for that use is necessary under the Town and Country Planning Act 1971 and has not been granted. Such a use becomes prohibited if, and only if, an enforcement notice is served, or if by other processes an injunction is granted against that particular use'.

As this case demonstrates, owners or developers cannot claim exemption from unoccupied rates on the grounds that the property has no valid planning permission. It is only when enforcement action is taken that exemption can apply.

The situation is not so clear as regards the question of whether exemption may be claimed in respect of a building which fails to meet the requirements of the Fire Precautions Act 1971 (as amended) regarding the provision of an adequate means of fire escape. The 1971 Act does not of itself prohibit the occupation of buildings that do not comply with the relevant statutory provisions – this occurs only when the fire authority obtains a court order. At this point exemption from unoccupied rates would apply. In a pre-court order situation, however, although a person may be guilty of an offence if he occupies a property without a satisfactory means of escape and with no valid fire certificate, such unlawful occupation might not have been expressly prohibited and thus the exemption from unoccupied rates would not apply (see *Regent Lion* above).

Some of these issues were addressed in *Tower Hamlets London Borough Council v St Katherine-by-the-Tower Ltd* [1982] RA 261. The case concerned the fifth floor of Europe House; it was occupied by the Port of London Authority which was exempt from the London Building Acts and therefore it did not have to have a means of fire escape. On their vacating the fifth floor (on 31 March 1979), the respondents were obliged to provide an approved means of fire escape if they wished to let the premises. Plans were approved and the necessary work was completed by the end of August 1980. The rating authority applied to the magistrates' court for a distress warrant for unoccupied rates for the fifth floor for part of 1979–1980 and 1980–1981. The respondents argued that no unoccupied rates were payable by virtue of paragraph 2(a) of Schedule 1 to the General Rate Act 1967, which provided that 'no rates shall be payable for any period during which (a) the owner is prohibited by law from occupying the hereditament or allowing it to be occupied'. The magistrates' court refused to issue the distress warrant, and the rating authority appealed to the High Court. The High Court confirmed the decision of the lower court.

In another case, *Hailbury Investments Ltd v Westminster City Council* [1986] 1 WLR 1232, it was claimed that a property was unoccupied by virtue of the effect of a planning condition making use of the premises a breach of condition. The issue was whether the ratepayers were entitled to exemption from liability. The House of Lords held that as the ratepayers were not prohibited from occupying the hereditament, they were therefore liable to unoccupied rates.

(c) The hereditament is kept vacant by reason of action taken by or on behalf of the Crown, or any local or public authority, with a view to prohibiting the occupation of the hereditament or to acquiring it.

This might cover, for example, the preliminary run-up to clearance areas (unfit property), and it also appears to cover those situations where a blight notice could be sustained.

(d) The hereditament is the subject of a building preservation notice (listed building) as defined by section 58 of the Town and Country Planning Act 1971, or is included in a list compiled under section 54 of that Act. (These are now contained in the Planning (Listed Buildings and Conservation Areas) Act 1990.)

Where a building is 'listed' as prescribed above, and currently vacant, exemption from unoccupied property rates will be conferred.

However, where part only of a building is listed, in what way does exemption apply, if at all? In *Providence Properties Ltd v Liverpool City Council* [1980] RA 189, a hereditament consisted of three warehouse buildings, of which only one was listed. The company contended that the hereditament was exempt from unoccupied rates, but this contention was rejected. The legislation, where it referred to 'hereditament', did not infer or apply to a part of the hereditament. However, in *Debenhams plc v Westminster City Council* [1987] AC 396 the House of Lords investigated fully the dilemma posed where the hereditament (for rating purposes) covered more than the listed part. It seems likely that where the 'non-listed' part is an 'object or structure fixed to a building or forming part of the land and comprised within the curtilage of a building', it will be treated as part of the listed building and exemption will be granted. In the *Debenham's* case, their lordships found that a single hereditament which comprised two distinctly separate buildings (one of which was listed), and which were linked by a bridge and tunnel, was not entitled to exemption since only part of the hereditament was listed. The unlisted building could not be described as a 'structure'; the word is intended to be confined to such structures as are ancillary to the listed building itself, and does not include a stand-alone building.

Where a hereditament comprises an 'old' part which is listed and a 'new' part which is unlisted: if the 'old' part is let and a separate rating assessment is put on the 'new' part, then whilst that new part remains vacant, there is likely to be a liability for unoccupied property rates. If the position is reversed, in that the 'new' part is let, but the 'old' part remains vacant, then with regard to the 'old' part there will not be any liability for empty rates.

(e) ***The hereditament is included in the Schedule of Monuments compiled under section 1 of the Ancient Monuments and Archaeological Areas Act 1979.***

(f) ***It is a qualifying industrial hereditament.***

The regulations define these hereditaments in broadly the same terms as were contained in the Rating (Exemption of Unoccupied Industrial and Storage Hereditaments) Regulations 1985 (SI 1985 No 258). An **industrial hereditament**, as defined in the Non-Domestic Rating (Unoccupied Property) Regulations 1989, means any hereditament other than a retail hereditament (see below) in relation to which all buildings comprised in the hereditament are:

(i)   constructed or adapted for use in the course of trade or business; and

(ii) constructed or adapted for use for one or more of the following purposes, or one or more of such purposes and one or more purposes ancillary thereto:

- manufacture, repair or adaptation of goods or materials, or the subjection of goods or materials to any process;
- storage (including the storage or handling of goods in the course of their distribution);
- the working or processing of minerals; and
- the generation of electricity.

The question of what constitutes 'storage' was considered in *Barnet London Borough Council v London Transport Property* [1995] EGCS 78. The council argued in the magistrates' court that London Transport was liable to pay non-domestic rates for a bus depot. The magistrate found that although some repairs were carried out in a small part of the hereditament, the primary purpose of the parking area was for the accommodation of buses when not in use. In the opinion of the magistrate this accommodation amounted to 'storage', and therefore the hereditament qualified for exemption. A case was stated to the High Court which allowed the council's appeal, concluding that it was necessary to consider the nature of the activity involved, namely the overnight accommodation or parking of buses at the depot. The judge went on to comment that if the buses had been decommissioned, and were being kept at the premises awaiting disposal, there would have been force in the argument that they were being 'stored'. However, storage did not include parking of the buses when that was an integral part of their normal daily operation. They were in active use and it was a necessary incident of that use that they should be parked whilst not in use or between periods of use. The buses were therefore not being stored within the context of the regulations.

Retail hereditament means any hereditament where any building or part of a building comprised in the hereditament is constructed or adapted for the purpose of the retail provision of:

  (i)   goods; or
  (ii)   services, other than storage for distribution services, on or from the hereditament.

This definition excludes a hereditament from unoccupied property rates relief where any building, or even part of a building, is constructed or adapted for retail purposes. It will be of interest to see how this section will be applied to those situations where the hereditament is industrial but has a small retail element, for example, a factory shop. A possible simple solution might be to treat the whole hereditament as industrial and therefore exempt, given that the shop may be incapable of being treated as a separate unit of occupation. However, if the sales shop were in a separate building, it is possible that the whole hereditament will not qualify for exemption, given that the hereditament does not comply with the criterion that '... all buildings comprised in the hereditament are ...'.

(g)   *Properties whose rateable value in the new local rating list is less than £1,500.*

(h)   *Properties where the owner is entitled to possession only in his capacity as the personal representative of a deceased person.*

(i)   *There subsists in the owner's estate a bankruptcy order under the Insolvency Act 1986.*

(j)   *The owner is entitled to possession of the hereditament in his capacity as a trustee under a deed of arrangement under the Deeds of Arrangement Act 1914.*

(k)   *The owner is a company which is subject to a winding up order made under the Insolvency Act 1986.*

(l)   *The owner is entitled to possession of the hereditament in his capacity as liquidator by virtue of the Insolvency Act 1986.*

In essence the only true new category relates to small hereditaments whose rateable value shown in the rating list is less than £1,500.

However, an important special rule has been made under section 65(5) of the LGFA 1988 which treats as unoccupied a hereditament which would otherwise be treated as occupied by reason *only* of there being kept in or on the hereditament plant, machinery or equipment, provided, and this is critical, that it was used in the hereditament when it was last in use or it is intended for use in the hereditament. This section, which largely re-enacts section 46A of the General Rate Act 1967, is designed to apply to those hereditaments which have closed down, but plant, machinery or equipment have remained in the hereditament and which could therefore attract occupied property rates liability. In such circumstances the payment of occupied property rates would be a very heavy burden. The section also applies to a new building, thereby reversing the decision of the House of Lords in *British Telecommunications v Kennet District Council* [1983] RA 43, in which it was held that telephone exchanges were in rateable occupation during the installation of telephone equipment within the newly completed buildings.

A further case on this point was *Sheafbank Property Trust plc v Sheffield City Metropolitan District Council* [1988] RA 33, where it was held that a sports ground and premises must be treated as unoccupied by virtue of section 46A of the General Rate Act 1967, because the proper approach to the section was for the rating authority to ask itself, whether, but for the presence of plant, machinery or equipment, it would have found occupation, and the only matter which (but for s 46A) could have resulted in the appellant company being rateable was the presence of the contents which were accepted by the rating authority to be plant, machinery or equipment and so must be disregarded.

Also under section 65(6), those hereditaments used only to hold public meetings by parliamentary candidates, and rooms used by election returning officers, are to be treated as unoccupied.

3. Part occupation

Where a hereditament is only partly occupied, this from the ratepayer's point of view can create some difficulties if he wishes to try and reduce his liability to reflect the unused part. The general rating principle of 'occupation of the part is occupation of the whole' can in many cases be justifiably applied; however in other cases it can lead to unfairness. With regard to partly unused non-domestic hereditaments there are two possible courses of action.

First, where the unoccupied part is likely to remain so for a long period of time it may be possible for the ratepayer to request a subdivision of the hereditament to create separate hereditaments. In such circumstances the uses of each part are important in that each part must be used for a wholly different purpose, as was found in *North Eastern Railway Co v York Union* [1900] 1 QB 733. The use and non-use of a building can be treated as two different purposes. Having established the different uses, each part must then be capable of separate occupation. In *Moffat v Venus Packaging Ltd* (1977) 243 EG 391, the hereditament was a factory complex which was partly in occupation, but which had several buildings vacant. The tribunal found that as the vacant part was separated from the occupied part and as each part had a different use (occupation and non-occupation being held to be different uses) and was capable of being let separately, the parts were entitled to be treated as separate hereditaments.

The second approach is at the discretion of the billing authority which can in certain circumstances implement the provisions contained in section 44A of the LGFA 1988. They broadly replicate the provisions of section 25 of the General Rate Act 1967. Section 44A allows a simplified process for providing for a reduced payment of rates on an unoccupied part of a building when it is likely to be unoccupied for only a short time. The pre-conditions to the operation of the section are that it must appear to the billing authority that part of a hereditament is unoccupied, and that this will remain so for a short time only. This is primarily a question of fact; there is no guidance on what is meant by 'a short time'. It could be argued that it might mean more than three months – and possibly more than one year – given that the end of one financial year and the beginning of the next brings one apportionment to an end and grounds for the application of a new apportionment. These provisions allow for the billing authority to request the valuation officer to apportion the rateable value of the hereditament between the occupied and unoccupied parts, provided that the part unoccupied will remain so for a 'short time' only. It is not envisaged that there will be provisions for appeal against the valuation officer's apportionment. This is an important change from the previous system which required that the apportionment had to be agreed between the authority and the occupier.

There are constraints within which the apportionment must operate. For a new apportionment, the operative period begins on the day on which the hereditament became partly unoccupied; in the case of a further apportionment, the operative period begins on the day on which that apportionment took effect. The apportionment remains valid until one or more of the following events occur:

(a)   the occupation of the unoccupied part;

(b)   the end of the rate year for which the authority requires the apportionment;

(c)   the requiring of a further apportionment;

(d)   the hereditament becomes completely unoccupied.

The constraint in (b) above means that after 31 March in each year any apportionment that is operative ceases to have effect. If the billing authority wishes to continue the arrangement in the following rate year, it must use its discretion to require a further apportionment. It is likely that the valuation officer's earlier certificate will stand if there have been no material changes.

An additional regulation is to be introduced to allow these provisions to apply retrospectively; this was not possible under the previous statutory powers.

4. Completion notices

With the introduction of unoccupied rating it became necessary to introduce a procedure for establishing when unoccupied newly erected or altered buildings could be regarded as completed for rating purposes, so as to activate liability to empty rates. This saw the introduction of completion notices, now governed by section 46A and Schedule 4A to the LGFA 1988 as amended by paragraph 36 of Schedule 5 to the Local Government and Housing Act 1989.

The use of completion notices allows billing authorities to bring quickly within the scope of the business rate provisions those buildings which have undergone extensive refurbishment, or newly erected buildings. The purpose of a completion notice is to establish with the person entitled to possession of a relevant hereditament the date from which the building is to be treated as completed. From that date the three month rate-free period begins. It was held in *Watford Borough Council v Parcourt Property Investment Co Ltd* [1971] RA 97 that a building remained a newly erected building until first occupied, and in order for there to be liability to unoccupied rates a completion notice must be served. It mattered not whether the hereditament was entered in the valuation list; without a completion notice, no empty rates could be charged (see *Drake Investments Ltd v Lewisham London Borough Council* [1983] RVR 150).

Billing authorities are required by paragraph 1 of Schedule 4A to the LGFA 1988 to serve on the owner/ratepayer a completion notice as soon as it comes to their attention that the work remaining to be done can reasonably be expected to be done within a period of three months. The completion notice may be served on the whole building or only a part of it. In order to meet this requirement, authorities will liaise with the valuation officer as to whether a building or part of it is capable of being entered in the rating list.

Completion notices must specify the date considered by the authority as one by which the building could reasonably be completed, and which must not be more than three months from the date of service of the notice. In the case of a building where the work remaining to be done is of a type which is customarily carried out after the building has been substantially completed, the time reasonably required to do that work is added to the date on which the building was substantially completed, thereby deferring the final date of completion. The phrase 'such period ... as is reasonably required for carrying out the work' does not include the time for finding tenants willing to occupy the building who may then decide what form the outstanding work should take (see *JGL Investments Ltd v Sandwell District Council* [1977] RA 78), or the period likely to be required to obtain statutory permissions and approvals, for example planning permission, fire certificates etc. In *London Merchant Securities plc and Others v London Borough of Islington* [1988] AC 303, [1987] 3 WLR 173, the House of Lords had to consider when a modern office development was to be treated as completed so as to fix the date when unoccupied property rates would become payable. Relevant to the case were the answers to the following questions: first, what kind of work is customarily done to a building of this type *after* substantial completion and secondly, what period of time is reasonably required for carrying out the customary work which remains to be done? In *Ravenseft Properties Ltd v Newham London Borough Council* [1976] QB 464, [1976] 2 WLR 131, the issue was whether a newly erected office block was on the date specified in the completion notice a completed building. The main structure was completed, but the building had no internal partitioning, no telephone installation, and the electrical installation was incomplete. As it stood, the building was incapable of occupation as offices. Bridge LJ said:

'If the building lacks features which before it can be occupied will have to be provided and when provided will form part of the occupied hereditament and form the basis of valuation of that hereditament, then I would take the view, unless constrained to the contrary, that the building was not within the meaning of the relevant provision a completed building.'

This decision essentially followed the precedent in *Watford Borough Council v Parcourt Property Investment Co Ltd*.

If the ratepayer agrees with the completion date specified in the notice and signifies that agreement in writing to the authority, the completion notice is deemed to have been withdrawn.

In those cases where the ratepayer cannot demonstrate to the satisfaction of the authority that the building can be completed by the specified date, and the owner agrees a revised date in writing, the completion notice is deemed to have been withdrawn. Where the authority cannot agree a revised completion date the original completion notice may be withdrawn and a subsequent notice served with a revised completion date, but this power is not available if the ratepayer has appealed against the original completion notice and does not consent in writing to the withdrawal and re-service.

In some situations where a building is complete and a completion notice has not been served, the authority should attempt to agree a completion date, and failing that, issue a completion notice, with the completion date being the date of service of the notice.

In other circumstances the valuation officer may be aware of a completed building with no completion notice served. Here the valuation officer can attempt to agree the completion date with the ratepayer and enter the hereditament in the rating list. If he is able to reach formal agreement with the ratepayer, he must notify the authority of this action and direct the authority not to serve a completion notice.

Whilst the position under the old system was clear – no liability without completion notice – much confusion has arisen regarding the provisions of the LGFA 1988. *Prima facie* liability arises when the conditions in section 45 are fulfilled and in particular when the hereditament is entered in the list. The Department of the Environment Practice Note No 2 (para 3.8) gives clear guidance that if a valuation officer has been unable to agree a completion date with a ratepayer, he will bring the completion of the building to the attention of the billing authority which will then be required to issue a completion notice.

However, some valuation officers, but by no means all, point out that their general duty to maintain a list is not affected by the Practice Note, which is for guidance only and of no statutory effect. This duty must, in their opinion, include entering in rating lists new vacant buildings which they consider to be complete, with no need to await the issue of a completion notice.

It is considered that such an approach carries risks for all, not least the authority. Although section 46A specifically provides that where a day is determined under completion notice procedures, the hereditament will be deemed to become unoccupied on that day, no similar provision exists in section 45, that a hereditament will be deemed to become unoccupied on the day that it is first shown in the rating list. Furthermore, the absence of any physical item or the defective operation of a significant item in the building will not be 'corrected' without a completion notice. This could result in a nominal value being ultimately determined on, say, a new vacant office building with a defective heating or air-conditioning system.

Leaving aside these practical aspects, it is considered to be highly unlikely that Parliament ever intended that the extensive procedures it established for completion notices on new vacant properties should be so easily circumvented by some valuation officers. It is worth noting that when it comes to appeals regarding completion notices, valuation officers are not even a party.

Until such time as the present confusion is resolved, it is thought advisable for billing authorities to use the completion notice procedure to avoid the possible risks of perhaps losing two or three years' empty rates.

As previously stated, a completion notice can be served on part only of a building. However, any service of such completion notices should take into account the type of building and the continuing works in the remainder of the building. It seems reasonable that completion notices should not be served if the continuing works would substantially interfere with the completed part. For example, a single floor of a multi-storey building will not generally be the subject of a completion notice unless it can be beneficially occupied as a separate unit of accommodation and with no interference with the occupancy.

(a) Appeals against completion notices

In those situations where the authority and the owner are unable to agree a completion date and the authority serves a completion notice, the ratepayer can appeal to the Valuation Tribunal (VT) within twenty-eight days of the service of the notice. During this period of twenty-eight days the authority should attempt to reach agreement; if agreement is reached before the VT hearing, the appeal is deemed to have been withdrawn.

An appeal to the VT will consider factual information or written representations from the ratepayer and the charging authority. The VT, in determining the completion date, may confirm the date shown in the completion notice or may substitute any other date.

The VT is required to give a reasoned decision, copies of which are sent to all parties to the appeal. If the VT determines a date different from that shown in the completion notice, it seems that regulations will provide for financial adjustment including interest payable for the overpayment of unoccupied property rates.

A further right of appeal against the decision or order of the Valuation Tribunal can now be made to the Lands Tribunal (reg 47 Non-Domestic Rating (Alteration of Lists and Appeals) Regulations 1993 (SI 1993 No 291)). The appeal must be made within four weeks of the date on which notice is given of the decision of the VT. The Lands Tribunal has the power to confirm, vary, set aside, revoke or remit the decision or order of the VT, and may make any order the VT could have made.

(b) Summary

The effective date of an entry of a new or altered building in the local rating list will be:

(i)   the agreed date as the date of completion; or
(ii)   the date determined by the VT or higher court; or
(iii)   the date shown in the completion notice which has not been agreed or appealed against.

5. Constructive vandalism

Constructive vandalism or soft-stripping is now being seen by the owners of vacant commercial property as a possible method of escaping unoccupied rates. The process is not always straightforward or a guarantee of escaping liability. However, three tests have emerged which should result in the desired effect:

(i)   that the building be rendered incapable of beneficial occupation; and
(ii)   that it would require a prohibitive amount of expenditure to bring it back into use; and
(iii)   the works would take longer than three months to complete.

The soft-stripping could involve the removal of such installations as heating and air-conditioning plant and equipment, suspended floors and ceilings, trunking, ducting, pipes, cables, wiring, plumbing, partitions, kitchen equipment and sanitary ware. However, it should be realised that this work of destruction can often lead to problems of building and public liability insurance, debris disposal and the continuing deterioration of the fabric of the building.

It is not the intention of the authors to recommend this approach.

Chapter 5

Composite hereditaments

Relevant legislation:

- Local Government Finance Act 1988;
- Local Government and Housing Act 1989;
- Local Government Finance Act 1992;
- Non-Domestic Rating (Caravan Sites) Regulations 1990 (SI 1990 No 673);
- Non-Domestic Rating (Caravan Sites) (Amendment) Regulations 1991 (SI 1991 No 471);
- Council Tax (Situation and Valuation of Dwellings) Regulations 1992 (SI 1992 No 550);
- Non-Domestic Rating (Definition of Domestic Property) Order 1993 (SI 1993 No 542);
- Council Tax (Situation and Valuation of Dwellings) (Amendment) Regulations 1994 (SI 1994 No 1747).

1. Introduction

With effect from April 1993, Council Tax replaced all three forms of the Community Charge – the Personal Community Charge, the Standard Community Charge and the Collective Community Charge. Council Tax is a return to a property-based tax whilst still retaining a personal element built into the computation. The tax applies only to dwellings situate in the area of a billing authority and is payable by the resident or owner.

The basic principle is that owners/occupiers of domestic property are liable for Council Tax, whereas occupiers of non-domestic property are liable for rates. There will be cases where a decision has to be made as to whether property is, or is not, domestic, or whether it is part domestic and part non-domestic.

2. Council Tax

Council Tax is based on the capital value of domestic property, a significant change from the old rating system which assessed domestic property for rates on hypothetical rental values. The introduction of capital values had been advocated for many years as a means of overcoming the shortcomings of the previous system in terms of lack of open-market rental information and taxpayer comprehension. The Layfield Committee, in its review of local government finance in 1976, had stated:

> '... Capital value is now the best measure we have of the benefit people derive from the occupation of their houses. We therefore conclude that the rating system, if it is to continue, will have to be on the basis of capital value for domestic property.'

The amount of Council Tax payable depends upon the band to which the property is assigned. The Local Government Finance Act 1992 created eight different valuation bands for England and Wales. For England the bands are as follows:

Value not exceeding £40,000	A
Value exceeding £40,000, but not exceeding £52,000	B
Value exceeding £52,000, but not exceeding £68,000	C
Value exceeding £68,000, but not exceeding £88,000	D
Value exceeding £88,000, but not exceeding £120,000	E
Value exceeding £120,000, but not exceeding £160,000	F
Value exceeding £160,000, but not exceeding £320,000	G
Value exceeding £320,000	H

Domestic property: Whether something is domestic property is important for the purpose of determining:

- whether someone is to be subject to a billing authority's Council Tax; and
- whether the property is non-domestic and therefore liable to business rates.

The definitions of dwelling/domestic property are given separately under the respective legislation for Council Tax and non-domestic rating. The two definitions are essentially the same, as one would expect in view of the fact that they are endeavouring to identify the same object, namely that part of the property which is domestic.

Definition of dwelling for Council Tax purposes: Section 3(2) of the Local Government Finance Act 1992 provides the definition of dwelling as being any property which:

(a) would have been a hereditament for the purposes of section 115(1) of the General Rate Act 1967; and

(b)   is not shown or required to be shown in a local or central non-domestic rating list; and

(c)   is not exempt from local non-domestic rating for the purposes of Part III of the LGFA 1988.

Under section 3(4) none of the following property:

(i)   a yard, garden, outhouse or other appurtenance belonging to or enjoyed with property used wholly for the purposes of living accommodation; or

(ii)   a private garage which either has a floor area of not more than 25 square metres or is used wholly or mainly for the accommodation of a private motor vehicle; or

(iii) private storage premises used wholly or mainly for the storage of articles of domestic use,

is a dwelling except in so far as it forms part of a larger property which is itself a dwelling by virtue of section 3(2).

Definition of domestic property for non-domestic rating purposes:
Section 66 provides a wider definition of domestic property, and treats property as domestic if:

(a)   it is used wholly for the purposes of living accommodation;

(b)   it is a yard, garden, outhouse or other appurtenance belonging to or enjoyed with property falling within (i) above;

(c)   it is a private garage which either has a floor area of 25 square metres or less, or is used wholly or mainly for the accommodation of a private motor vehicle;

(d)   it is private storage premises used wholly or mainly for the storage of articles of domestic use.

The difference between the two definitions is not materially significant. The inclusion of 'used wholly for the purpose of living accommodation', within the non-domestic rating definition, is a recognition of the principle that rating is a tax on occupation and *per se* use.

Minor non-domestic uses: It is important to understand what 'wholly' used for living accommodation means, as regards other minor or occasional uses of the same property. In terms of use 'wholly' does not mean 'exclusively', which by inference allows some unimportant non-domestic use of the domestic property without affecting the status of the property as domestic. In certain cases the *de minimis* rule is applicable. Although in each case its application ultimately depends on the facts, it might be appropriate to consider the following:

- the effect of the frequency of the non-domestic use; and
- any alterations made to the property to facilitate that use.

For example, the front room of a dwelling-house which is used occasionally for non-domestic purposes such as hair-dressing (see section 66(2A)) does not contravene the 'wholly used' requirement so as to bring the property into non-domestic rating. On the other hand, a spare room in a dwelling might have been converted to accommodate a solarium or be used as a veterinary sugery. In these cases it is likely that the property will be treated as a composite and will therefore require two assessments.

Vacant property: Section 66 provides that property not in use will be treated as domestic if it appears that when next in use it will be used domestically.

In this context, 'appears' encompasses more than just the physical attributes of the property. For example, if an unconverted shop used as a residence is worth considerably more as a residence than for any permitted business use, it would be unlikely that, when vacant, a future use other than domestic could reasonably be expected. Accordingly in such a clear-cut case, the property, when vacant, will not attract a liability for empty non-domestic property rates. However, in less obvious cases, the physical attributes of a property might determine whether it is rated when it falls vacant.

3. Identification and valuation

(a) Identification of composite hereditaments

A hereditament which is neither used wholly for domestic purposes nor wholly for non-domestic purposes is essentially a 'composite hereditament'. This term was first introduced by section 68(9) of the LGFA 1988, and roughly corresponds to 'mixed hereditament' under the old system. The test for identifying a composite hereditament is the use to which it is put. If the hereditament is wholly used for domestic purposes, even if as 'vacant and to let' it would be capable of non-domestic use, it must be excluded from business rate assessment. If it is wholly used for non-domestic purposes, it is liable for business rating only.

A composite hereditament is defined in section 64(9) as a hereditament part only of which consists of domestic property. By virtue of section 64(1), 'hereditament' has the same meaning as it had under the General Rate Act 1967, namely 'property which is or may become liable to a rate, being a unit of such property which is, or would fall to be, shown as a separate item in the valuation list'.

Clarification on the essential elements of a single hereditament can be gained from a study of the leading cases, such as *Gilbert v Hickinbottom* [1956] 2 QB 240, [1956] 2 WLR 952. The key element is 'one occupation', which can be affected either by all parts actually being occupied by one person or by a body corporate – the latter including occupation by employees and agents.

Therefore it can be said that it is in the nature of a composite hereditament that both its domestic and non-domestic parts are occupied by the same ratepayer.

Once a hereditament has been identified as composite, then by virtue of section 64(8) it is classed as non-domestic and must be included in the rating lists. Although the whole hereditament is entered on the rating list, the rating assessment relates only to the non-domestic use. The entry in the list is qualified by the addition of the word 'part' to the description.

(b) Valuation of the non-domestic part of composite hereditaments

Paragraph 2(1) of Schedule 6 sets out the general basis for determining the rateable value of a non-domestic hereditament:

'The rateable value of a non-domestic hereditament shall be taken to be an amount equal to the rent at which it is estimated the hereditament might reasonably be expected to let from year to year if the tenant undertook to pay all usual tenant's rates and taxes and to bear the costs of repairs and insurance and the other expenses (if any) necessary to maintain the hereditament in a state to command that rent.'

For composite hereditaments, paragraph 2(1A) provides:

'The rateable value of a composite hereditament shall be taken to be an amount equal to the rent which, assuming such a letting of the hereditament as is required to be assumed for the purposes of sub-paragraph (1) above, would reasonably be attributable to the non-domestic use of the property.'

Additionally, paragraph 2(3) and (4) gives effect to the valuation prepared at the antecedent valuation date, 1 April 1993. However, as with many other parts of the new legislation, the Secretary of State may amend the basis of valuation and prescribe new rules.

For a composite hereditament, by virtue of paragraph 2(1A) above, it is the whole hereditament which is deemed to be vacant and to let and the whole hereditament is to be valued, but the rateable value to be shown in the rating list is limited to the value attributable to the non-domestic use only. Additionally, the legislation qualifies the attributable non-domestic value with the word 'reasonably'. Following the consultation paper on the valuation of composite hereditaments issued in February 1989, the Government decided that the valuation approach should be on the basis of a notional distribution of uses.

It is felt that the use of the qualification 'reasonably' will admit the notional basis approach to defining the physical limits of the non-domestic part. However, where this notional basis is at variance with the actual distribution of uses, it may be necessary to prove the 'reasonableness' by reference to the actual distribution within similar hereditaments nearby.

Having arrived at the 'definition' of the non-domestic part, the rent of the entire hereditament is then apportioned to the non-domestic part. This will ensure that any advantages or disabilities (such as the condition of the structure, disrepair or poor access) affecting the whole hereditament are reflected in the rated part, and also avoids the problems that could have arisen by adopting a different approach to the definition of the rating unit – for example, if the domestic element was deemed 'not to exist', what would have been the effect on the value when there were toilet facilities within the domestic part which were available to and used with the non-domestic part?

The tremendous permutation of types of possible composite hereditaments, and the balance of uses within those types, precludes any simple guidance to the valuation approach other than to examine carefully the actual uses existing and whether this is a reasonable balance of uses.

Two examples might help to demonstrate some of the practical problems which can be encountered. Firstly, with regard to a residential school which also caters for day pupils, the approach would be to value the whole school and then to apportion the value between the excluded residential components and the remaining non-domestic parts. This would mean that residential accommodation used exclusively by boarders and residential staff would be excluded. Shared accommodation, such as kitchens and dining areas, would require apportionment. Similarly, there would be apportionment in respect of facilities shared by residents and non-residents, such as playing fields, tennis courts and swimming pools.

Secondly, with regard to hotels, there is likely to be residential accommodation for staff. Staff bedrooms, kitchens and rest-rooms would all need to be excluded from the non-domestic rating assessment. However, where rest-rooms etc. are also used by day staff, an apportionment would be required.

(c) Valuation of the domestic part of composite hereditaments

Regulations 6 and 7 of the Council Tax (Situation and Valuation of Dwellings) Regulations 1992 (SI 1992 No 550) require the capital valuation of the entire composite hereditament. This is known as 'the relevant amount'. Thereafter the valuer proceeds with identifying that portion of the relevant amount which can reasonably be attributed to domestic use of the hereditament.

It will be appreciated that, for example, a three-bedroom caretaker's flat within a large office block may make little discernible difference to the capital value of the entire building, thereby warranting an entry within Band A. This would be the correct approach notwithstanding that, just around the corner, there are similar sized self-contained flats selling at prices which vindicate their entries within, say, Band G.

4. Examples

The following examples are intended to give some insight into the treatment of domestic property and the interrelationship between the Council Tax and non-domestic rating.

(a) Shops with living accommodation

These will normally be treated as composite hereditaments, if the flat is occupied with the shop, entailing the valuation of the non-domestic part only. The following are a number of hypothetical examples:

(i) A shop wholly occupied for non-domestic purposes, the upper floors being used for storage purposes, will be entirely non-domestic and entered in the rating list.

(ii) Another shop is occupied on the ground floor for non-domestic purposes, with the upper floors being used for living accommodation. A number of other shops in the parade are similarly occupied. Valued vacant and to let, its actual occupation is in accord with its expected notional occupation and therefore only the ground floor will be assessed for business rates.

(iii) A shop similar to (ii) above, except that a ground floor store-room is used for domestic purposes. No structural alterations have been made; vacant and to let, it is unlikely that the hypothetical tenant would occupy the property in this way. The notional test applies, and the property will be assessed as in (ii) above.

(iv) A shop like (iii) above, except that the ground floor store is structurally severed from the non-domestic part. In this case the actual physical condition overrides any question of notionality. Therefore only the non-domestic part will be assessed for business rates.

(b) Factories/offices with living accommodation

(i) A caretaker's flat in an office block will normally be his sole residence and will be treated as domestic and will not be business rated: the occupier should pay the relevant Council Tax.

(ii) A flat provided by a company as the sole residence of the chairman or director will be domestic.

(c) Private garages and private storage premises

The first point to note is that there is no statutory definition of either 'private garage' or 'private storage premises'; however a private garage is to be treated as domestic and is not business rated provided that either:

(i) it has a floor area of 25 square metres or less; or

(ii) if the floor area exceeds 25 square metres, it is used wholly or mainly for the accommodation of a private vehicle.

If the garage qualifies under (i) above, it is irrelevant what type of vehicle it houses. However, under (ii) the type of vehicle is important: if it is a commercial vehicle, such as a taxi, lorry or van, the garage will be liable to non-domestic rating. A case in point is *Andrews (VO) v Lumb* [1992] RA 124, which was concerned with whether a warehouse and premises should be classed as domestic or non-domestic.

The building was used for the storage, maintenance and restoration of vintage vehicles, principally old buses, and for the storage of items of transport memorabilia. It was held by the Lands Tribunal that the premises were non-domestic, because the articles being stored there could not be described as articles of domestic use.

77

Where a garage is being used for some purpose other than for housing a vehicle, for example as a workshop, it is treated as rateable irrespective of its size. If this use is short-term or *de minimis*, it can be ignored. In *Walker v Lothian Region Assessor* [1990] RA 283, a private store contained tools, timber, workbenches and other equipment previously used by the appellant in a commercial venture. The Scottish Lands Tribunal held that the property was non-domestic and was therefore properly included in the valuation roll. This was primarily because the storage of workbenches and timber was not shown to be ancillary to, or wholly in connection with, domestic property.

With regard to storage premises, if the articles stored are of a domestic nature, the premises qualify as private storage under the provisions of section 66 and are not rateable.

(d) Hotels and guest houses

These hereditaments continue to be liable for non-domestic rates, as was the case before 1 April 1990. This includes the bedrooms for short-term lettings, public rooms, dining rooms, kitchens, bars, offices etc. However, accommodation within the premises provided for the proprietor and family will be domestic.

Accommodation for others, such as long-term guests, students or homeless people, will be domestic property and will be treated as those people's sole or main residence. Unfortunately there are no clear definitions of 'short-term' – which attracts rating liability – and 'long term' – which attracts the Council Tax.

(e) Seasonal occupation

Seasonal premises which are closed out of season will normally remain in non-domestic rating, this being no different to the situation before 1 April 1990. However, in certain circumstances the ratepayers can secure the removal of the entry from the local rating list for part of the year and so avoid liability for rates. This can happen if the valuation officer is satisfied that the accommodation has reverted to domestic use, as would be the case of a private dwelling-house which offers bed and breakfast on an occasional basis and whose bedrooms previously used by guests have now reverted to the owner's private use. In addition, liability for rates will cease if the accommodation is used by students or homeless prople for whom it is their sole or main residence. Premises used for seasonal non-domestic purposes will not be assessed or appear in the rating lists until non-domestic use actually occurs. When the seasonal non-domestic use comes to an end, the ratepayer is entitled to have the list entry deleted.

(f) Short-stay accommodation

Short-stay accommodation, and its entitlement to exemption or liability for non-domestic rates, has been the subject of considerable debate. It is accepted that if a person makes a limited use of his own house to provide short-stay bed and breakfast accommodation, this would normally be considered *de minimis* and would not give rise to any liability for non-domestic rates. However, if a house is used for the whole of the summer to provide such short-stay accommodation, clearly there is justification to rate the property.

Regulations SI 1990 No 162 (Standard Community Charge and Non-Domestic Rating (Definition of Domestic Property) Order 1990) were therefore passed, providing an exclusion of liability for properties which were used for bed and breakfast accommodation for fewer than 100 days a year. This 100-day rule was subject to much criticism, including the fact that it was possible to evade liability since the test based on the 'intent' of owners to offer accommodation for more or less than 100 days. The Government accepted the shortcomings of the 100-day test, but still argued that short-stay accommodation offered beyond what could be construed as *de minimis* should be liable for non-domestic rates. The Department of the Environment issued a Guidance Note on 1 April 1991, which stated that:

> 'If you offer bed and breakfast accommodation in your own home to six people or less you are exempt from non-domestic rates, provided the bed and breakfast use is subsidiary to the residential use.'

The Standard Community Charge and Non-Domestic Rating (Definition of Domestic Property) Order 1990 (SI 1990 No 162) amended section 66(2) of the LGFA 1988 in respect of the definition of domestic property. In its amended form section 66(2) now reads:

> '(2) Property is not domestic property if it is wholly or mainly used in the course of a business for the provision of short-stay accommodation, that is to say accommodation –
>
> (a) which is provided for short periods to individuals whose sole or main residence is elsewhere, and
>
> (b) which is not self-contained self-catering accommodation provided commercially.'

By the Standard Community Charge and Non-Domestic Rating

(Definition of Domestic Property) (Amendment) Order 1991 (SI 1991 No 474), section 66(2) was further amended as follows:

'(2A) Subsection (2) above does not apply if –

(a) it is intended that within the year beginning with the end of the day in relation to which the question is being considered, short-stay accommodation will not be provided within the hereditament for more than six persons simultaneously; and

(b) the person intending to provide such accommodation intends to have his sole or main residence within that hereditament throughout any period when such accommodation is to be provided and that any use of living accommodation within the hereditament which would, apart from this subsection, cause any part of it to be treated as non-domestic, will be subsidiary to the use of the hereditament for, or in connection with, his sole or main residence.'

Therefore, under this new 'six person rule', the intention must be ascertained of the person providing the accommodation. In addition, a 'subsidiarity' rule has been introduced, its effect being that any other use of the hereditament should be subsidiary to the use of the hereditament as the occupier's sole or main residence – see *Hodkinson v Humphreys-Jones (VO)* [1995] RA 314 and 364–366.

The interpretation of section 66(2A) arose in *Skott v Pepperell (VO)* [1994] RA 326. This case was concerned with whether a hereditament should be treated as domestic and therefore exempt from non-domestic rates, or whether it was in fact a composite hereditament, with the part of the hereditament used as a guest house to be treated as non-domestic. On the facts the tribunal found that the provision of *en suite* facilities in all the bedrooms that were occupied commercially, and the provision of a fire alarm system and emergency lighting all went beyond that which would be provided in a private residence. The tribunal concluded that the accommodation provided to individuals for short periods in the part of the hereditament that was used as a guest house was not subsidiary to the use of the hereditament as the appellant's sole or main residence. Consequently exemption under section 66(2A) did not apply.

(g) Self-catering accommodation

Self-catering accommodation which is not self contained or let commercially is covered by section 66(2B) of the LGFA 1988 and is valued as non-domestic property. If accommodation of this type is occupied as a sole or main residence, then liability for non-domestic rates ceases, resulting in the creation of a composite hereditament or the removal of an entry from the local rating list.

If the accommodation is self contained and self catering, but not let commercially, it is still treated as non-domestic and the 140-day rule which applies to commercial self-catering accommodation does not apply (see *(h)* below).

(h) Commercially let self-contained self-catering accommodation

This type of living accommodation is covered by section 66(2B) of the LGFA 1988 which applies if the property is:

    (i)   available for letting for short periods;
    (ii)   available to individuals whose sole or main residence is elsewhere;
    (iii) self contained;
    (iv) self catering; and
    (v)   let on a commercial basis.

For accommodation which meets the above requirements, if:

    (i)   the number of days on which it is available is greater than 140 days in a year, the accommodation is subject to non-domestic rating for the whole year;
    (ii)   it is intended that the availability for occupation is to be less than 140 days, the person to whom the accommodation belongs will be liable to Council Tax;
    (iii) the accommodation is occupied by a person and is treated as his sole or main residence, that person will be liable for Council Tax.

The test to be applied is one of intention rather than actual letting, and the 140 days do not have to be consecutive.

(i) Public houses

Accommodation used as the sole or main residence of the owner or manager will be domestic. Rooms to let for short-stay guests will be treated in the same way as hotel rooms.

(j) Hospitals, nursing homes and old people's homes

Within institutions like these, living accommodation which is a person's sole or main residence will give rise to Council Tax.

Hospital wards, operating theatres, laboratories and accommodation for short-stay patients whose sole or main residence is elsewhere will be treated as non-domestic.

(k) Schools and universities

Houses and flats for teaching and administrative staff will be domestic, as will be halls of residence. However, use of halls by conference residents could give rise to non-domestic rating.

Non-domestic use usually applies to assembly halls, classrooms, laboratories, libraries and recreational facilities.

(l) Houseboats and moorings

A mooring will be domestic property if it is occupied by a boat which is someone's sole or main residence. Where the boat is not a sole or main residence, the mooring alone will be assessed for business rates. In theory, if a boat which was subject to Council Tax becomes vacant, its use would change to non-domestic. At this point it has to be considered whether the vacancy is short term and whether the next use is likely to be domestic. If domestic appliances and furniture remain on the boat, it is reasonable to assume that the next use will be domestic (s 66(5) LGFA 1988).

In *Turner v Coleman (VO)* [1991] RA 1, premises including a mooring, land and chalet were originally assessed as non-domestic. On appeal to the Lands Tribunal the valuation officer conceded that the chalet fell to be treated as domestic property, because articles of a domestic nature were stored in it. However, it was held by the tribunal that the mooring and land should be non-domestic since none of the paragraphs of section 66(1) was satisfied, it being pointed out that the property was not enjoyed with the occupier's residence which was some 1.25 miles away.

(m) Caravans

Touring caravans for use on holiday will not attract liability for Council Tax or non-domestic rates.

A static caravan which is someone's sole or main residence will attract Council Tax liability. If it is not a sole or main residence the pitch on which the caravan stands and the caravan itself will be subject to non-domestic rating – see the Non-Domestic Rating (Caravan Sites) Regulations 1990 (SI 1990 No 673), and the Non-

Domestic Rating (Caravan Sites) (Amendment) Regulations 1991 (SI 1991 No 471).

(n) Timeshares

With effect from 1 April 1993, section 66 of the LGFA 1988 was amended by the Non-Domestic Rating (Definition of Domestic Property) Order 1993 (SI 1993 No 542) which stated that property is not domestic property if it is timeshare accommodation within the meaning of the Timeshare Act 1992. Timeshare property, whether occupied or vacant, will therefore be subject always to non-domestic rates.

(o) Chalets and beach huts

The liability of a holiday chalet or beach hut to either Council Tax or non-domestic rates will depend upon a number of factors. One of the main points to be considered is whether the property provides living accommodation for someone's sole or main residence – if so, Council Tax will apply. Beach huts which provide a place to leave personal clothing for short periods are unlikely to be considered as living accommodation, and will be liable to non-domestic rating (see *Marks v Eastaugh (VO)* [1991] RA 4 and 5).

Holiday chalets, if they are considered to be living accommodation, could be subject to the same tests as other self-contained, self-catering accommodation. If the owner's intention is to let the property for short periods amounting to 140 days or more in a year to individuals whose sole or main residence is elsewhere, business rates will be payable. If the property is let commercially for less than 140 days per year, or is used as a second home, the owner would be subject to Council Tax. If it is not let commercially, it would be treated as self-catering accommodation (see *(g)* above).

5. Summary

The following is intended to give some indication of what type of property is likely to fall within which category:

Domestic:

- residential unit (used wholly for the purposes of living accommodation);
- yard, garden, outhouse or other appurtenance;
- caravan pitch (and van) licensed for year-round residential occupation, or which is the sole or main residence;

- mooring occupied by a boat which is the sole or main residence;
- unused property which, when next occupied, will be domestic;
- hospitals for long-stay patients;
- hostels for full-time students;
- rehabilitation centres;
- religious houses (monasteries and convents) – also part exempt.

Composite hereditaments:

Non-domestic occupations where there is also occupation by full-time residents, or staff, for example:

- hospitals for short-stay patients or outpatients;
- hostels for short-term residents;
- hotels;
- boarding houses;
- offices or factories with permanent accommodation for caretakers or identified directors;
- boarding schools;
- public houses;
- shops with living accommodation.

Non-domestic:

- holiday caravan parks;
- holiday camps;
- blocks and complexes of self-catering units;
- time share complexes;
- beach huts.

Chapter 6

Rateable value and repairs

Relevant legislation:

- Local Government Finance Act 1988 (Sch 6);
- Local Government and Housing Act 1989 (Sch 5 para 38).

The value of property for rating purposes has always been the annual rent or annual value which could reasonably be achieved for the hereditament. The first definition of net annual value was enacted in section 1 of the Parochial Assessments Act 1836. In 1862, section 15 of the Union Assessment Committee Act introduced gross value. The main distinction between net annual value and gross value was that for gross value the responsibility for repairs and insurance was moved from the hypothetical tenant to the hypothetical landlord. In 1925, section 68 of the Rating and Valuation Act specified the classes of hereditaments which were to be assessed to gross value, leaving net value for the remainder. The consolidating legislation of the General Rate Act 1967, as well as clarifying the classes or types of hereditaments appropriate to the different approaches, also provided that for those properties valued to gross value, rateable value was to be arrived at by a set scale of deductions; whereas, for the remainder, rateable value was to be the same as net annual value.

It was realised by the late 1970s that in any future revaluation of non-domestic hereditaments, any basis other than a full repairing and insuring one would be inappropriate, given the general pattern of repairing obligations in open market lettings.

Accordingly, from 1 April 1990, all non-domestic property has been required to be valued direct to rateable value. Paragraph 2(i) of Schedule 6 to the LGFA 1988 defines rateable values:

'The rateable value of a non-domestic hereditament ... shall be taken to be an amount equal to the rent at which it is estimated the hereditament might reasonably be expected to let from year to year if the tenant undertook to pay all usual tenant's rates and taxes and to bear the cost of repairs and insurance and other expenses (if any) necessary to maintain the hereditament in a state to command that rent'.

Within that definition, the part relating to repairs requires some interpretation since no two properties are likely to be in the same condition, even if they are in the same location and used for the same purpose. This could present difficulties from two angles: first, on the actual rent passing and its usefulness in arriving at the base level or 'tone' in revaluation; secondly, the part it may play in an initial decision to appeal against an assessment and the arguments on that appeal.

The majority of business leases provide that the tenant must keep the demised space in repair during the currency of the tenancy. This is often backed up by a further covenant to render up in good repair at the end of his tenancy. At the commencement of a tenancy, there will be occasions when both parties recognise that the property is in poor condition and a low initial rent will reflect this – often accompanied by specific covenants by the tenant to carry out specific works.

The possible permutations are appreciated by the Valuation Office Agency. An examination of the Forms of Return used by the office illustrates the care taken to identify the factors which may necessitate an adjustment to the actual rent passing on a particular property.

But what standard of repair is to be envisaged or assumed? Clearly prime offices in a city's business core will enjoy a higher standard of repair than, say, a workshop on an old industrial estate nearing the end of its economic life.

Guidance can be found in *Anstruther-Gough-Calthorpe v McOscar* [1924] 1 KB 716; although it was not a rating case, it was concerned with the interpretation of a repairing covenant. It was referred to in the case concerning the assessment of Brighton Pier (*Brighton Marine Palace and Pier Co v Rees* [1961] RVR 614). In the 1924 case, Banks LJ said:

'the cost of putting the premises ... into such condition as I should have expected to find them in, had they been managed by a reasonably minded owner, having full regard to the age of the buildings, the locality, the class of tenant likely to occupy them and the maintenance of the property in such a way that only an average amount of annual repair would be necessary in the future'.

This still provides a useful checklist in deciding an appropriate standard of repair for any hereditament. But how should one approach the situation in which a hereditament's physical condition is clearly below this appropriate standard? Under the previous legislation, with the majority of properties being assessed to gross value, a considerable body of case law was built up establishing tests for the hypothetical landlord's repairing obligations. The Court of Appeal decisions in *Wexler v Playle* [1960] 1 QB 217 and *Saunders v Maltby* (1976) 239 EG 205 – both of which were concerned with dwellings in disrepair – established that where a property assessed to gross value was in disrepair, the proper consideration, *per* Lord Denning, was:

> 'Whether the disrepair was such that it would be reasonable in all the circumstances to expect a hypothetical, reasonable landlord to do the repairs. If the cost of doing the repairs would be out of all proportion to the value of the house ... then it must not be assumed that he would do them. Rather, he would let the premises at a low rent. In those circumstances the low rent would be the basis on which to arrive at the value'.

The economic test was also adopted and developed in *Sanz v Dudbridge* [1980] RVR 204. In considering the correct assessment for a dwelling in disrepair, the Lands Tribunal after reviewing the various items and their costs, decided that although some clearly fell within the reasonable hypothetical landlord's obligations and were therefore deemed to have been remedied, others did not. The Member reduced the assessment by 15 per cent to reflect only these items.

What is the position where all the repairing obligations are transferred from the hypothetical landlord to the hypothetical tenant? It has been suggested that the two words can just be interchanged and all the previous case law under gross value can be applied to a rateable value approach, i.e. for 'landlord' read 'tenant'. This cannot be correct: how can an annual tenant, even with a reasonable prospect of continuing his tenancy, fulfil the economic test applied to the hypothetical landlord by Lord Denning? Additionally, under the gross value approach, once it was decided that items of disrepair fell within the 'reasonable hypothetical landlord' test, not only was their existence to be disregarded but so also was the disruption to occupation while they were being remedied. Consequently, if very real doubts exist about an annual tenant being subject to an economic test, he can neither be deemed to put the premises in good repair at the commencement of his tenancy, nor can his predecessor (under the same tenancy terms) be presumed to have put the hereditament in good repair at the end of his hypothetical tenancy. Additionally, when significant works of repair are actually being carried out, it can be argued that their interference with the enjoyment of the hereditament should warrant a lower assessment.

One of the few cases which looked at the question of disrepair in a hereditament valued direct to rateable value was *Snowman Ltd v McLean* [1979] RVR 284, 251 EG 859, where the Lands Tribunal had to consider the correct assessment for a factory in Harrow which suffered from cracks and differences in floor levels. The original rateable value assessment of £12,400 was reduced by the Lands Tribunal by 10 per cent; the Member stated in his decision that the hypothetical tenant, on seeing the defect, would have reduced his bid so as to allow for above-average repairs; in addition, having sought the advice of an expert, he would have been concerned about the risk of further work being needed with its consequential extra financial burden and interruption of occupation. The tribunal specifically rejected the valuation officer's arguments that (i) it could be assumed that the outgoing tenant would have remedied the defects, and (ii) the hypothetical tenant would not have sought specialist advice.

Brighton Marine Palace and Pier Co v Rees [1961] RVR 614 concerned the assessment of Brighton pier. The Lands Tribunal considered at length questions of repairs, renewals, sinking funds and insurance. Because of the nature of the hereditament, however, it was agreed on all sides that it should be valued on a profits approach. Consequently, on all of these points, the case was concerned with looking at the accounts of the actual operators to see whether the sums expended would be in line with the amounts that a hypothetical tenant would allow. Although such considerations are unlikely to be relevant to the majority of hereditaments, the decision does contain useful comment upon the required standard of repairs and the distinction between repairs and renewals. Additionally, in commenting upon the likely approach to the insurance of such an unusual property, the Lands Tribunal did distinguish between the likely attitudes and responses of an owner-occupier and a tenant from year to year.

In Northern Ireland the onus to repair has always been the responsibility of the tenant under the definition of net annual value as contained in Part I of Schedule 12 to the Rates (Northern Ireland) Order 1977. There have been a number of decisions on the effect of disrepair on net annual value. *McCann v Commissioner of Valuation* VR/33/1989 concerned a cottage in poor structural condition with excessive damp. The repairs were beyond the repairing

obligations of the tenant and the question was whether the hypothetical landlord would have repaired the defects. The tribunal held
that the hypothetical landlord would have let it in its actual state at
a reduced rent.

In rating law the concept of *rebus sic stantibus* is important, ensur-
ing that the value follows the existing state of things and not the
potential or possibility of how things might be in the future. When
valuing to gross value, this rule was considerably modified for
disrepair by Lord Denning's 'reasonable landlord' approach. It is
unlikely that, with the new system of valuing direct to rateable
value, such a degree of modification to the rule will be accepted.

No doubt the Lands Tribunal will have to consider these matters
extensively in the not-too-distant future. It is hoped that early guidance will be given, or a host of appeals will arise on both the
disrepair question and on the question of assessment when serious
disrepair is being rectified.

Chapter 7

Valuation date and 'tone of the list'

Relevant legislation:

- Local Government Finance Act 1988;
- Local Government and Housing Act 1989 (Sch 5);
- Rating Lists (Valuation Date) Order 1992 (SI 1992 No 1643);
- Non-Domestic Rating (Material Day for List Alterations) Regulations 1992 (SI 1992 No 556).

1. The General Rate Act 1967

Under the previous system there was no statutory provision fixing the date of valuation for rating purposes. Sections 19 and 20 of the General Rate Act 1967 merely set out the basis of valuation, described the approach to be adopted, and identified admissible or relevant circumstances.

However, case law clearly established that valuations under section 19 were to be as at the date of the originating proposal. In *Barratt v Gravesend Assessment Committee* [1941] 2 KB 107, the divisional court considered the assessment of a public house, and determined that the date of the proposal was the correct date and not the beginning of the rate period in which the proposal was made (which had previously been thought to be the correct approach). Since war had commenced during the rate year in question, the ratepayer obtained a reduced assessment for a few months preceding the start of the war.

It was not until the case of *K Shoe Shops v Hardy* [1983] 1 WLR 1273 that valuations under section 20 of the General Rate Act 1967, and by inference the list itself, were clearly stated to take effect from the date the list came into force. This case concerned the assessment of a shop in Regent Street, London. Although the parties had agreed what the value was at April 1973, the ratepayer's agents argued for a lower assessment based upon the apparent 'tone' of agreed values for nearby streets which it was contended showed a valuation date of several years earlier. In rejecting the ratepayer's arguments, the House of Lords decided that the only logical valuation date must be the date the list came into force, i.e. 1 April 1973.

With section 20 valuations, the longer a list lasted, the greater the problems of the 'mental gymnastics' needed to project circumstances back from the proposal date to the year preceding that when the list came into force – particularly so for types of properties and locations which had not existed in 1972. Additionally, much debate and case law in the 1980s sought to clarify what circumstances existing at a later proposal date could properly be reflected in a notional 1972/73 base.

The culmination came with the House of Lords' decision in *Addis v Clement* [1988] 1 WLR 301, which was concerned with the admissibility of the effect of the designation of an enterprise zone in Swansea – with rates 'holidays' for properties inside the zone – on the value and assessment of properties outside the zone. The leading judgment of Lord Keith put a wide construction on valuations under section 20 so as to include intangible (i.e. economic and legal) as well as physical advantages and disadvantages. However, within a very short time, that unanimous Lords' decision was reversed by the enactment of section 121 of the LGFA 1988, which effectively restricted section 20 valuations to a consideration of the proposal date physical factors or physical manifestations.

2. The Local Government Finance Act 1988

Once it had been decided that a revaluation would come into effect in 1990 and that there was to be a firm commitment to subsequent regular revaluations the legislators addressed the problems concerning valuation date (fixing the 'tone' or level of values), the admissible circumstances or physical factors affecting that valuation and, finally, whether there was any need for valuations under section 19 for subsequent falls in value due to matters other than the admissible physical factors.

(a) Antecedent valuation date

Since it was expected that the new lists would take some two years to prepare, and in order to avoid the evident problems of having to project likely rental levels from the preparation period to the date when the lists would take effect (1 April 1990), it was decided that the valuation date would be 1 April 1988. For the 1995 lists the valuation date has been set at 1 April 1993 – this fixes the level and pattern of values for the 1995 lists. The statutory authority for an antecedent valuation date is contained in paragraph 2(3) of Schedule 6 to the LGFA 1988, and the date of 1 April 1993 was fixed by the Rating Lists (Valuation Date) Order 1992 (SI 1992 No 1643).

However, in the preparation of the lists, the physical condition and 'setting' of the hereditaments were to be taken as the day the lists were compiled and came into force (1 April 1995). This element of projection could not be avoided.

Therefore, although the rating valuation is based on values prevailing at the antecedent valuation date, conditions prevailing at 1 April 1995 are taken into account as regards the physical state of the hereditament, the locality and other properties in the locality. The introduction of the antecedent valuation date necessitated the introduction of statutory provisions to deal with those situations where circumstances changed between 1 April 1993 and 1 April 1995.

These are contained in paragraph 2(5) of Schedule 6 to the LGFA 1988:

'where the Rateable Value is determined for the purposes of compiling a list by reference to a day specified under sub-paragraph (3)(b) above, the matters mentioned in sub-paragraph (7) below shall be taken to be as they are assumed to be on the day on which the list must be compiled (1 April 1995)'.

The 'mentioned matters' are set out in paragraph 2(7) of Schedule 6 as follows:

'(a)   matters affecting the physical state of the hereditament;

(b)   the mode or category of occupation of the hereditament;

(c)   the quantity of minerals in or extracted from the hereditament;

(cc)   the quantity of refuse or waste material which is brought onto and permanently deposited on the hereditament;

(d)   matters affecting the physical state of the locality in which the hereditament is situated, or which though not affecting the physical state of the locality, are nonetheless physically manifest there, and

(e)   the use or occupation of other premises situated in the locality of the hereditament.'

The wording of paragraph 2(7) emphasises the physical aspects regarding both the subject hereditament and the locality in which it is situated. Clearly, therefore, matters which are not 'mentioned' must be taken as they actually existed at the antecedent valuation date, and this includes financial and other economic aspects. The actual rates payable, whether high or low, can be envisaged only as those existing at the antecedent valuation date – therefore any appeal using an 'equation' argument would have only a very remote chance of succeeding. At its simplest, the 'equation' argument envisages a single pot of money being available for rent and rates. If, after a revaluation, considerably more has to be paid in rates, the argument runs that less money would be available for, or offered in, rent.

Some of the terms in 'mentioned matters' are either self-explanatory or use the same wording as was used in previous legislation. For example, 'mode or category of occupation' was fully considered in *Midland Bank v Lanham* [1978] RA 1 and in *S & P Jackson Ltd v Hill* [1980] RA 195.

The expressions, however, merit further consideration.

(i) 'the use or occupation of other premises situated in the locality'

It should be noted that this wording is different from that used in respect of the hereditament itself ('mode or category'). It not only includes the fact that hereditaments are used and occupied but also the vacancy of those other hereditaments. The 'quality' of occupation (e.g. the fact that a national retailer has moved out of premises which have then been reoccupied by a local discount trader) is likely to be relevant also.

'Locality' is not defined in the legislation; it was touched on in the *K Shoe Shops* case (see above) but it will be different for different classes of hereditament: the distance of any source of change, use or vacancy affecting a value for a motorway service area, for example, is likely to be very different from that affecting a warehouse or shop.

(ii) 'physical state or physical enjoyment of the hereditament'

Alterations to the hereditament itself clearly affect the physical state, both during and after their being carried out. Subject to the statutory repairing assumptions (see Chapter 6), this expression may also cover the hereditament being in disrepair or when repairs are being carried out.

The physical enjoyment of the hereditament may be affected by the presence or absence of certain services within the hereditament or, for example, by building works in progress to the building of which the hereditament forms part.

Allowances for building works nuisances, both internal and external are likely to remain as significant a part of appeals as they were for lists compiled under the General Rate Act 1967, provided that they have an effect on rent and subject to the 'cancelling' effects of the transitional arrangements.

(iii) 'physical state of the locality, or which ... are nonetheless
    physically manifest there'

'Physical state' obviously includes such factors as new competing shopping developments, changes in the number or size of car parks, pedestrianisation schemes, and clearance/demolition schemes.

'Physically manifest there' has already generated significant debate and is likely to provide much argument and litigation. It clearly covers the availability and 'quality' of public transport and parking restrictions, but it probably does not cover the pricing policy of existing parking, bus or rail services. A pricing policy is not 'physically manifest'.

Future events might also come under this heading, if there is a very real prospect of their occurring during the life of the hypothetical tenancy, since all matters that would affect the rental bid of the hypothetical tenant must be reflected. In *Dawkins (Almond) v Ash Brothers and Heaton Ltd* [1969] 2 AC 336, the House of Lords held that a demolition order, which was likely to take effect within a year of the relevant date, was a factor which the hypothetical tenant would properly have regard to and would accordingly offer a reduced rent.

* * *

It must be stressed, however, that in the Government's opinion the wording for 'mentioned matters' solely encompasses physical conditions and circumstances and that it was drafted at the same time as *Addis v Clement* was being reversed by statute.

All these changes, and particularly the antecedent valuation date, are a considerable improvement over the previous system which projected values ahead when preparing the list. There is still the problem, in some cases at the very beginning of the new lists, of the level of values from one period being applied to the different physical circumstances of another period – for example there might be a change in circumstances between the antecedent valuation date and the date when the list comes into force. To minimise argument, valuation officers have made extensive use of still and video photography of major shopping streets, centres and individual hereditaments to 'fix' the physical factors at, or close to, the antecendent valuation date.

(b) Material day

When the rateable value of a hereditament is being considered after the list has come into force, under paragraph 2(6) of Schedule 6 the 'mentioned matters' are taken to be those existing on the 'material day' – which essentially clarifies the valuation date. Material day is defined by the Non-Domestic Rating (Material Day for List Alterations) Regulations 1992 (SI 1992 No 556).

(i) Where the alteration is to correct an inaccuracy in the list on the day on which it was compiled, the material day is the day on which the list was compiled (reg 3(2) SI 1992 No 556).

(ii) Where an alteration is made to correct an inaccuracy in the list which arose in the course of making a previous alteration or is occasioned by a proposal disputing the accuracy of a previous alteration, the material day is the day by reference to which the 'mentioned matters' fell to be considered when determining the rateable value with a view to making the alteration which gave rise to the inaccuracy, or the accuracy of which is disputed (reg 3(3)).

(iii) (a) Where the alteration is made in order to insert into or delete from the list any hereditament which:

● has come into existence or ceased to exist; or

● has ceased to be, or become, required to be shown in the central rating list; or

● has ceased to be, or become, part of the relevant authority's area by virtue of a change in that area; or

(b) Where the alteration is made in order to insert into or delete from the list any hereditament or part of a hereditament which has ceased to be, or become, domestic property or property exempt from non-domestic rating,

the material day is the day on which the circumstances giving rise to the alteration occurred (reg 3(4) and (6)).

(iv) In relation to an unoccupied newly erected property, the material day is either the day proposed in the completion notice as the completion day, or, where a completion day has been agreed or determined, the day so agreed or determined (reg 3(5)).

(v) In any other case, the material day is the day on which the proposal for the alteration is served on the valuation officer, or, if there is no such proposal, the day on which the valuation officer alters the list (reg 3(7)).

Chapter 8

Transitional arrangements

Relevant legislation:

- Local Government Finance Act 1988 (ss 57 and 58 and Sch 7A);
- Local Government and Housing Act 1989 (Sch 5);
- Non-Domestic Rating (Chargeable Amounts) Regulations 1994 (SI 1994 No 3279);
- Non-Domestic Rating (Chargeable Amounts) (Amendment) Regulations 1995 (SI 1995 No 961).

1. Introduction

Before 1 April 1990, the only provision for ratepayers withholding part of their full rate payment was under section 8 of the General Rate Act 1967. This applied only to those cases where ratepayers had appealed against their new rating assessment within six months of a revaluation taking effect, and entitled them to withhold 50 per cent of the difference between the old and new (higher) rate bill until such time as the appeal was finally settled.

The Yellow Paper, *Paying for Local Government*, which was issued in July 1987, proposed that this should be done away with and replaced by (i) a ceiling on the increase in rateable values, (ii) large increases in rates bills resulting from the combined effect of the revaluation and the uniform or national rate, to be phased in over a maximum of five years with an upper limit on the year-on-year percentage increase, and (iii) interest payable at a rate determined by the Secretary of State when an overpayment of rates was refunded following a successful appeal.

The first of these proposals never reached the statute book. This chapter is concerned only with the transitional arrangements or the phasing-in of new rates bills when they are significantly above or below the previous year's bills.

Although the detailed legislation is complex, and was subject to much amendment during the life of the 1990 list, the general aim can be expressed simply as providing that no occupier's rate bill may increase annually by more than a set percentage plus inflation. However, since the changes have always been intended to be 'revenue neutral' – i.e. to have no effect on the aggregate revenue – the limitation on increases is paid for by a limitation on decreases. The provisions are contained in section 57 and Schedule 7A to the LGFA 1988 (as amended) and in orders and regulations made under the Act. They originally applied from the beginning of the 1990/91 financial year to the end of the 1994/95 financial year. Under section 58 of the LGFA 1988, new provisions could be introduced after 31 March 1995 to deal with revaluations. These are now enacted by virtue of the 1994 Regulations.

2. 1990 list transitional arrangements

The 1994 Regulations recognize (reg 5) that even some five years after the 1990 revaluations there may be some hereditaments whose rate bills were still subject to 'phasing' in the 1994/95 financial year. It is therefore necessary to have a brief understanding of the previous regulations as they could still have an effect on a ratepayer's rate liability in 1995/96 and beyond.

As originally enacted, the transitional arrangements applied to defined hereditaments – assessed in the 1973 valuation lists and in the 1990 local rating lists – with a further occupational qualification for those hereditaments facing increased rate bills. The effect of this latter aspect was that although the phasing of decreases 'ran with the property', the phasing of large increases was personal to a particular occupier and ceased upon a change of occupation.

Following significant protests during the first two years, when some rate bills increased by more than 60 per cent and there were complaints about distortion of the property market, phasing of increases – other than inflation – was suspended for 1992/93 and 1993/94. Additionally, the provision restricting the phasing of increases to qualifying occupiers was scrapped in 1992 and all phasing in of decreases was scrapped from 1 April 1993.

3. 1995 list transitional arrangements

There are four elements to the 1994 Regulations. Firstly, for phasing to apply, the hereditament must be a 'defined hereditament'. If it is not, then phasing will not apply. Three calculations must then be carried out. These are:

(a) the base liability (BL);

(b) the notional chargeable amount (NCA); and

(c) the appropriate fraction (AF).

Each of the above and 'defined hereditaments' are explained in the following paragraphs but, before doing so, it is worth noting that, unlike the original 1990 Regulations, (i) phasing of increases does 'run with the property', and (ii) there is no lower rateable value limit to the phasing arrangements (for the 1990 list, this had been set at £500 rateable value).

4. Defined hereditaments (reg 3 and Schs 1 and 2 to the 1994 Regulations)

There are three categories of 'defined hereditaments';

(a) it was in the 1990 list on 31 March 1995, was in the 1995 list on 1 April 1995, and every day since; or

(b) it is an altered hereditament, wholly or mainly comprising property which appeared originally in either the 1990 or 1995 lists, and was deleted from either list as a result of structural alterations, and following the alterations is entered in the 1995 list; or

(c) it is a new hereditament arising from the division of an old hereditament into two or more parts; or from the merger of two or more old hereditaments into a single hereditament; or the reconstitution of two or more old hereditaments into two or more different hereditaments.

5. Base liability (regs 5, 6 and 7 of the 1994 Regulations)

Where a hereditament was still within the previous transitional provisions on 31 March 1995, the base liability for 1995/96 is to be calculated in accordance with regulation 5. Leaving aside complications caused by changes in value since 1 April 1990, or by splits and mergers, base liability in such a case is to be found by applying the formula:

$$(BL \times AF) \times 365$$

where:

BL is base liability for the hereditament for 31 March 1995 determined in accordance with paragraph 4(5) of Schedule 7A to the LGFA 1988; and

AF is the appropriate fraction for the hereditament for 31 March 1995 determined in accordance with paragraph 5(2) of Schedule 7A to the LGFA 1988.

Where a hereditament was outside the previous transitional provisions on 31 March 1995, the base liability for 1995/96 is to be calculated in accordance with regulation 6 which provides the formula:

$$Y \times Z$$

where:

Y is the rateable value shown for the hereditament on 31 March 1995; and

Z is the non-domestic rating multiplier for 1994/95.

For financial years subsequent to 1995/96, regulation 7 provides that the base liability for the relevant year shall be found by applying the formula:

$$(BL \times AF)$$

where:

BL is the base liability for the hereditament in the immediately preceding relevant year; and

AF is the appropriate fraction for the hereditament in the immediately preceding relevant year.

6. Notional chargeable amount (reg 4 of the 1994 Regulations)

This is effectively the amount of rates payable in any year if phasing did not apply.

Subject to special provisions relating to splits and mergers, altered hereditaments etc., regulation 4 provides that the notional chargeable amount for a defined hereditament for a relevant year is to be found by applying the formula:

$$A \times B$$

where:

A is the rateable value shown for the hereditament on 1 April 1995; and

B is the non-domestic rating multiplier for the relevant year.

For 1995/96, the rating multiplier – often referred to as the UBR – has been set for England and Wales at:

England   43.2p in £

Wales   39.0p in £

Further changes in the UBR will be limited to future movements in inflation.

(In the 1990 lists, Wales had a higher UBR than England. The relative change in the UBRs for England and Wales is a result of the changes in the aggregate rateable values in the rating lists for England compared with those for Wales.)

7. The appropriate fraction (reg 8 of the 1994 Regulations)

The appropriate fraction is the percentage limiting the rate of increase or decrease in rate liability. It is the product of the percentage factor prescribed in regulation 8 for the particular size of hereditament in a relevant year multiplied by the change in the retail price index over the defined period.

The formula for the appropriate fraction is stated in regulation 8 as:

$$\frac{X}{100} \times Q$$

Q is found by the formula $\dfrac{RPI(1)}{RPI(2)}$

where RPI(1) is the retail price index for September immediately preceding the relevant year and RPI(2) is the retail price index for September in the year before RPI(1). It is to be rounded to three decimal places.

Thus for 1995/96, Q will be:

$$\frac{\text{RPI September 1994}}{\text{RPI September 1993}} = \frac{145.0}{141.9} = 1.022$$

X in the formula in regulation 8 (see above) will vary according to whether the hereditament is a 'large', 'small' or 'small composite' hereditament and whether the notional chargeable amount is greater or less than the base liability.

A 'large' hereditament should be interpreted as one with a rateable value of £15,000 or more in Greater London (or £10,000 or more outside Greater London). A 'small' hereditament is one with a rateable value below these limits.

The prescribed 'X' factors are as follows:

(i)   for increases

	1995/96	1996/97*	1997/98	1998/99	1999/2000
large hereditaments	110	107.5	110	110	110
small hereditaments	107.5	105	107.5	107.5	107.5
small composites	105	105	105	105	105

reflecting November 1995 Budget (SI 1995 No 3322).

(ii)   for decreases

large hereditaments	95	95	85	70	70
small hereditaments	90	90	80	65	65

NB In respect of decreases, composites have the same X factor as large or small hereditaments, depending upon the actual rateable value.

The appropriate fraction for a large hereditament subject to a phased decrease in 1995/96 would therefore be:

$$\frac{95}{100} \times 1.022 = 0.9709$$

Similarly, for a small hereditament subject to a phased increase, the appropriate fraction for 1995/96 would be:

$$\frac{107.5}{100} \times 1.022 = 1.09865$$

8. Chargeable amounts

By virtue of regulations 9 and 10, the transitional arrangements are only applicable to defined hereditaments if:

(a)   NCA is greater than BL and greater than (BL × AF), or

(b)   NCA is less than BL and less than (BL × AF)

where:

NCA is the notional chargeable amount;

BL is the base liability; and

AF is the appropriate fraction —

all in respect of the hereditament for the relevant year.

Where the hereditament falls within the transitional arrangements under either of the above tests then the actual rates liability, i.e. the chargeable amount, is calculated by the formula:

$$\frac{(BL \times AF)}{C}$$

where C is the number of days in the year in which the relevant day falls.

It is only at this stage that reliefs applicable to charities or unoccupied property are brought into play, by dividing the chargeable amount – as calculated above – by 2, 5 or 10 as appropriate.

9. Special cases

(a) Vacant or partly occupied property

Regulations apply the transitional arrangements where empty rates only are payable (reg 10(6)).

(b) Charitable relief

Whether mandatory or discretionary, the relief is calculated after the transitional adjustment has been made (reg 10(4) and (6)).

(c) Splits and mergers

Regulations are in place to cover these eventualities. They are complex, and in every case reference should be made to the regulations themselves (Sch 2 1994 Regs).

(d) Changes in rateable value

Regulations deal with the calculation of the rates bills for changes in rateable vaue after 1 April 1995 or where there were physical changes affecting the property on 1 April 1995 (regs 11 and 14).

(e) Newly constructed hereditaments

With regard to newly constructed hereditaments (i.e. those genuinely first assessed on or after 1 April 1995), the transitional arrangements will not be applicable since they are not defined hereditaments. Many concerns have been expressed about the different treatment these hereditaments receive compared with altered hereditaments (see paragraph 4, above). There has also been criticism of the absence of clarity or definition in respect of the phrase 'wholly or mainly' when applied to altered hereditaments. When does major rebuilding amount to a new hereditament?

(f) Central list hereditaments

The 1994 Regulations (as amended by the 1995 Regulations) make special provision regarding the transitional arrangements for central list hereditaments. Regulations 18 to 26 contain the general provisions for calculating the chargeable amounts of defined central list hereditaments where the rateable value is assessed conventionally. Regulations 27 to 34 contain corresponding provisions in respect of central list hereditaments for which rateable values are prescribed.

Schedules 3, 4 and 5 contain further provisions regarding central list hereditaments which are being split or merged, or are being combined with local list hereditaments from 1 April 1995.

The detailed provisions of the central list regulations are outside the scope of this book as they are likely to be of interest to only a very limited number of ratepayers and their advisers.

(g) Crown hereditaments

Transitional arrangements apply to Crown hereditaments on an extra-statutory basis and are not the responsibility of the billing authority. Crown contributions and transitional relief are calculated by the Crown Property Unit, and are paid to the Secretary of State who credits the contributions to the national non-domestic rate pool.

Should a hereditament cease to be Crown property and no longer exempt from normal non-domestic rating, regulation 16 provides for the appropriate valuation officer to certify rateable values on any relevant day and on 31 March 1995.

(h) Special authorities

For the purpose of calculating the notional chargeable amount for an area deemed to be a special authority, the special authority multiplier should be used instead of the uniform business rate multiplier. The base liability is calculated in the normal way, but the transitional limit is calculated by adjusting upwards or downwards by the difference, if any (there is none in 1995/96), between the special authority multiplier and the uniform business rate multiplied by the 1 April 1995 rateable value (regs 12 and 13).

(i) Certification by valuation officers

It must be appreciated that not only hereditaments ceasing to be Crown property (see *(g)* above) fall to be certified under regulation

35, but there will also need to be certification by the appropriate valuation officer (i) in respect of splits or mergers effective on 1 April 1995, and (ii) – more contentiously – for altered hereditaments. With regard to (ii), the valuation officer will be required to certify what the value of the altered hereditament would have been on 31 March 1995 in its latest, altered condition.

All such certificates can be appealed against (reg 36); unless the notice of appeal is withdrawn or agreement is reached, appeals proceed in the normal way, being heard and determined by the Valuation Tribunal.

It should be borne in mind that the provisions are complicated. Although the Act and regulations do not lend themselves to easy analysis, reference should always be made to the legislation to ensure compliance in any specific case.

10. Examples

Example A – simple increase

An office building in Birmingham. Its rateable value in the 1990 list was agreed at £142,500 (applicable from 1 April 1990 to 31 March 1995) and it was not in the previous transition scheme at 31 March 1995. Its assessment in the 1995 list is £336,000 rateable value.

Calculation:

(i) Base Liability (BL) $= £142,500 \times 42.3p \ (Y \times Z)$
  $= £60,278$

(ii) Notional Chargeable
  Amount (NCA) $= £336,000 \times 43.2p \ (A \times B)$
  $= £145,152$

(iii) Appropriate Fraction (AF)

As there is an increase, and the hereditament is large – i.e. more than £10,000 rateable value outside Greater London – the appropriate fraction will be:

$$\frac{110}{100} \times \frac{1.022}{100} \ (X \times Q)$$

$$= 1.1242$$

(iv) NCA is greater than BL and also exceeds (BL × AF). Therefore the transitional limit (BL × AF) will apply.

(v) The chargeable amount will be:

$$£60,278 \times 1.1242$$
$$= £67,765$$

Note: £67,765 will become the base liability when considering the transitional arrangements for 1996/97.

Example B – simple reduction

An office building in the West End of London which was erected in the 1980s. It had an agreed assessment for the whole of the 1990 list at £500,000 rateable value. Its assessment in the 1995 list is £250,000 rateable value. It was not in the transitional scheme in 1994/95.

Calculation:

(i) Base Liability (BL) $= £500,000 × 42.3p (Y × Z)$
    $= £211,500$

(ii) Notional Chargeable
    Amount (NCA) $= £250,000 × 43.2p (A × B)$
    $= £108,000$

(iii) Appropriate Fraction (AF)
    As there is a decrease, and the hereditament is 'large' – i.e. more than £15,000 rateable value in Greater London – the appropriate fraction will be:

$$\frac{95}{100} × 1.022 \quad \frac{(X × Q)}{100}$$

$$= 0.9709$$

(iv) NCA is less than BL and is also less than (BL × AF). Therefore the transitional limit will apply.

(v) The chargeable amount will be:

$$£211,500 × 0.9709$$
$$= £205,345 \text{ (or £561.05 per day)}$$

Note:
- £205,345 will become the base liability when considering the transitional arrangements for 1996/97;
- the daily rate for 1995/96 is calculated by dividing by 366 (leap year).

Example C – merger of assessments after 1.4.95

Suppose that the hereditament in Example A is merged with another hereditament, C, on 2 October 1995. It had a rateable value on 1 April 1995 of £100,000 with a base liability of £18,200, NCA of £43,200, and a chargeable amount of £20,460 – all on an annual basis.

The merged hereditament is entered into the list at £400,000 rateable value. Paragraph 6 of Schedule 2 provides that the chargeable amount for a chargeable day is calculated by applying the formula:

$$\frac{R \times J}{S}$$

where: R is the aggregate of the previous daily chargeable amounts;

J is the new rateable value after merger; and

S is the aggregate of the rateable values before merger.

(based upon VO certificates, as appropriate).

(a) From 1 April 1995 to 1 October 1995

(i) Hereditament A

Daily chargeable amount = $\dfrac{£67,765}{366}$ = £185.15 per day

(ii) Hereditament C

Daily chargeable amount = $\dfrac{£20,460}{366}$ = £55.90 per day

(b) From 2 October 1995 to 31 March 1996

Merged hereditaments A and C

Daily chargeable amount = $R \times \dfrac{J}{S}$

$= £241.05 \times \dfrac{£400,000}{£336,000 + £100,000}$

$= £241.05 \times 0.9174$

$= £221.15$ per day

(c) Rate liability for occupier of A initially, and A and C subsequently in 1995/96, will therefore be:

(i) £185.15 × 183 days; and

(ii) £221.15 × 183 days.

Total liability = £74,325

Example D – division of assessment after 1 April 1995

Suppose that part of the hereditament in Example A is sublet, creating two hereditaments, D1 and D2, from 2 October 1995. They are entered in the list from that date with the following assessments – D1: £200,000 rateable value and D2: £70,000 rateable value. (The quantum allowance applicable to the original hereditament, whilst still applying to D1, is not reflected in D2.)

Paragraph 5 of Schedule 2 provides that the chargeable amount for a chargeable day is calculated by applying the formula:

$$\frac{R \times J}{S}$$

but in this case:

R is the chargeable daily amount for the 'old' hereditament before 2 October 1995, ignoring all reliefs;

J is the rateable value of the new hereditament; and

S is the rateable value of the 'old' hereditament.

(i) Hereditament D1

Daily chargeable amount $= £561.05 \times \dfrac{£200,000}{£250,000}$

$= £448.84$ per day

producing a rate bill from 2 October 1995 to 31 March 1996 of £82,138

(ii) Hereditament D2

Daily chargeable amount $= £561.05 \times \dfrac{£70,000}{£250,000}$

$= £157.09$ per day

producing a rate bill from 2 October 1995 to 31 March 1996 of £28,748

Note: The pro-rata increase in the rates burden for the small sublet part is not exceptional – there are even more dramatic examples to be found in the City of London.

Chapter 9

Billing, collection and enforcement

Relevant legislation:

- Local Government Finance Act 1988;
- Local Government and Housing Act 1989;
- Non-Domestic Rating (Collection and Enforcement) (Local Lists) Regulations 1989 (SI 1989 No 1058);
- Non-Domestic Rating (Collection and Enforcement) (Central Lists) Regulations 1989 (SI 1989 No 2260);
- Non-Domestic Rating (Collection and Enforcement) (Miscellaneous Provisions) Regulations 1990 (SI 1990 No 145);
- Non-Domestic Rating (Collection and Enforcement) (Local Lists) (Amendment) Regulations 1992 (SI 1992 No 1512);
- Non-Domestic Rating (Collection and Enforcement) (Central Lists) (Amendment) Regulations 1992 (SI 1992 No 1513);
- Council Tax and Non-Domestic Rating (Demand Notices) (England) Regulations 1993 (SI 1993 No 191);
- Non-Domestic Rating (Collection and Enforcement) (Amendment and Miscellaneous Provision) Regulations 1993 (SI 1993 No 774).

1. The chargeable amount

The rating multiplier (previously known as the rate in the pound) is no longer set by local authorities (except special billing authorities) – nor is it directly related to the projected expenditure of the billing authority. The non-domestic multiplier is set by the Secretary of State, and is then specified in the Revenue Support Grant Report which must be approved by resolution of the House of Commons. The multiplier is uniform throughout each country – hence the name Uniform Business Rate (but it should be noted that England and Wales still have their own, different UBRs) – except within those areas which are designated as special billing authorities and which have a discretion, within limits, to set their own multiplier.

The multiplier is determined in accordance with a formula which reflects changes in the retail price index. The Treasury has the power in certain instances to specify a lesser figure (Sch 7 paras 3 and 5 LGFA 1988).

(a) Multipliers

The multiplier for a year where there has not been a revaluation is calculated as follows:

$$\frac{A \times B}{C}$$

where A is the multiplier in the preceding financial year;

          B is the retail price index (RPI) for the month of September preceding the date on which the new multiplier takes effect;

          C is the retail price index for the September one year earlier.

Therefore, the multiplier which took effect in England on 1 April 1994 can be calculated as follows:

$$\frac{\text{1993/1994 multiplier for England} \times \text{RPI for September 1993}}{\text{RPI for September 1992}}$$

As can be seen from the formula, increases in the multiplier are limited to the rate of inflation as measured by the change in the RPI from September to September.

The multiplier, in a year of revaluation, is calculated by reference to the following formula:

$$\frac{A \times B \times D}{C \times E}$$

where A, B and C are the same as in the formula above, and

          D is the total rateable value in all local rating lists on the last day of the existing lists;

          E is the total of the rateable values on the first day of the new lists.

Therefore the multiplier for April 1995 can be calculated as follows:

$$\frac{\text{1994/95 Multiplier} \times \text{RPI for Sept 1994} \times \text{total rateable value on 31 March 1995}}{\text{RPI for Sept 1993} \times \text{total rateable value in new list on 1 April 1995}}$$

The following table illustrates the level of Uniform Business Rate for the financial years, to 1996:

Financial year	England	Wales	City of London
1990/91	34.8	36.8	34.8
1991/92	38.6	40.8	38.6
1992/93	40.2	42.5	40.2
1993/94	41.6	44.0	41.6
1994/95	42.3	44.8	42.3
1995/96	43.2	39.0	43.2
1996/97	44.9	40.5	44.9

2. Liability

A ratepayer is liable to non-domestic rating in respect of any day in the chargeable financial year if:

(a) on that day he is in occupation of all or part of the hereditament; and

(b) in respect of unoccupied hereditaments, on any day of a chargeable financial year none of the hereditament is occupied; and

(c) the ratepayer is the owner of the whole hereditament; and

(d) the hereditament falls within a prescribed class.

With regard to (d) above, for the purposes of unoccupied rating, the LGFA 1988 gives powers to the Secretary of State to prescribe classes of non-domestic hereditaments.

The amount which a ratepayer is liable to pay is calculated on a daily basis (ss 43 and 44 LGFA 1988), in accordance with a formula in which the only elements are the rateable value and the multiplier. The amount payable is calculated by reference to the following:

(i) the chargeable amount for each chargeable day; and

(ii) an aggregate of the daily amounts in (i).

(a) Occupied hereditaments

With regard to occupied hereditaments, the chargeable amount is calculated in accordance with the formula:

$$\frac{A \times B}{C}$$

where A is the rateable value shown in the rating list;
       B is the multiplier in force;
       C is the number of days in the financial year (either 365 or 366 days).

Example

A property is owner occupied and has a rateable value of £15,250 shown in the relevant local rating list. The chargeable amount will be:

$$£15,250 \text{ (A)} \times £0.348 \text{ (B)} = £5,307$$

The chargeable amount for each day becomes:

$$\frac{£5,307}{365 \text{ (C)}} = £14.53$$

If the occupier is in occupation on 1 April and then vacates the hereditament on 10 October, he will be liable for those days on which he was in occupation. This means that the day he vacated the premises is excluded from the calculation:

$$\text{Liability} = 192 \text{ days} \times £14.53 = £2,789.76$$

(b) Unoccupied hereditaments

Where a hereditament is shown in the local rating list and falls within a class specified by the Secretary of State and does not come within any of the exemptions to unoccupied rating, the amount payable is calculated by reference to the following formula:

$$\frac{A \times B}{C \times 2}$$

The amount of unoccupied rates chargeable is 50 per cent of the full rates payable. If the entitlement to the three month rate-free period has been used up, and the hereditament in the example above remains vacant for a full year, the chargeable amount is simply:

$$\frac{£15,250 \times £0.348}{2} = £2,653.50$$

or £7.26 per day

Where part of a hereditament is unoccupied, and will remain so for a short time only, the billing authority may request the valuation officer to apportion the rateable value of the hereditament between the occupied and unoccupied parts. The apportionment will apply to the operative period only, i.e. it begins on the day the hereditament is unoccupied and ends on the day it is reoccupied.

Where an apportionment is applicable to a hereditament which is not within a class specified as being subject to unoccupied rate liability, the chargeable amount is calculated by taking A, in the formula above, as the rateable value apportioned to the occupied part (s 44A(6) and (7) LGFA 1988). On the other hand, where the hereditament is within a class subject to unoccupied rates, the chargeable amount is calculated by taking the rateable value of the occupied part and adding it to half of the rateable value as apportioned to the unoccupied part (s 44A(8) and (9) LGFA 1988).

The apportionment lasts until:

- the occupation of any of the unoccupied parts;
- the ending of the rate period in which the authority requires apportionment;
- the need for any further apportionment of the hereditament; or
- the hereditament becomes completely unoccupied.

(c) Charities

Where the ratepayer is a charity, and it is accepted that the hereditament is wholly or mainly used for charitable purposes the formula for calculating the chargeable amount is the same as above – but with an allowance built in which gives the charity 80 per cent mandatory relief:

$$\frac{A \times B}{C \times 5}$$

Where the hereditament is vacant, but it appears that when next in use the hereditament will be wholly or mainly used for charitable purposes, the formula is:

$$\frac{A \times B}{C \times 10}$$

3. Billing and collection

The provisions governing the billing, collection and recovery of rates are contained within the principal regulations, Non-Domestic Rating (Collection and Enforcement) (Local Lists) Regulations 1989 (SI 1989 No 1058) (as amended), made by the Secretary of State under powers conferred by Schedule 9 to the LGFA 1988.

These regulations cover the important aspects of billing, collection and enforcement; the other regulations listed at the beginning of this chapter add to and amend the 1989 Regulations.

(a) Demand notices

The responsibility for billing, collection and recovery of rates lies with the billing authority; it is the charging authority which implements the new regulations in respect of the financial year which began on 1 April 1990.

In order to be liable for rates on any day, a person must be the owner or occupier of all or part of a hereditament included in the local non-domestic rating list. It is incumbent upon the billing authority to serve the demand notice or rates bill before it can legally begin to collect the rates; no rate is payable unless it has been properly demanded. A rate demand notice cannot be served until the billing authority has set amounts of Council Tax for the relevant year (reg 3 SI 1993 No 774). Where a demand notice is technically invalid because it does not contain all the legal requirements (see below), but the invalidity was due to a mistake and the amounts required to be paid were properly demanded in accordance with the principal regulations, the requirement to pay is enforceable. However, the billing authority is required to serve a further notice to correct the mistake.

Billing authorities must serve a separate rates bill for each year on every ratepayer liable for the rates. Where there is more than one occupier or owner of a hereditament at a particular time, they will be jointly and severally liable for the full amount of rates (regs 3 and 4 SI 1990 No 145). The interpretation of regulation 3 of SI 1990 No 145 was considered in *Ford v Burnley Borough Council* [1995] RA 205. In this case it was held that the occupier of part of a hereditament was not liable to an order for the whole of the rates, since it was not intended that the regulations should impose such a liability. The appellant traded from offices on the site of Ford Quarry in which other companies were also located. These companies were controlled by the appellant who had the major shareholding interest. The appellant paid the rates for the whole of the site, and then recouped the rates from whichever of the companies was doing best financially. The question before the court was whether the appellant, who was the occupier of part of a hereditament, justified a liability order against him on the ground that occupation of a part was, in the light of SI 1990 No 145, occupation of the whole. The court held that the regulations were intended to deal with joint occupiers of a hereditament, and did not impose on an occupier of part of a hereditament liability to pay rates on the whole of the hereditament. The liability order was therefore quashed.

The billing authority must serve a demand notice in respect of each hereditament. Where more than one hereditament is occupied by the same ratepayer, a single demand notice may be served to cover all the hereditaments. A composite bill like this must show the individual amounts due in respect of each hereditament and the statutory or agreed payment programme.

The demand notice must contain those matters specified in regulation 3(3) and Schedule 2 of SI 1993 No 191:

(i)   the address and description of the hereditaments;

(ii) the rateable value of each hereditament;

(iii) the non-domestic rating multiplier applicable for the relevant year;

(iv) a statement of the period during which, for the purposes of calculating the amount due, the property was unoccupied (note that with regard to the unoccupied period the chargeable amount is 50 per cent of the occupied rate);

(v) a statement of the period during which the ratepayer was or would be eligible for mandatory or discretionary charitable relief; or that the chargeable amount will be affected by the transitional provisions or the provisions relating to partly occupied property;

(vi) a statement of the manner in which the chargeable amount was calculated, reflecting any reduction or increase in the amount.

With the demand notice the billing authority must include certain explanatory information. This information consists principally of a description of the rating system, and includes such matters as rateable value, rating list, non-domestic rating multiplier, transitional arrangements and composite hereditaments (Sch 2 SI 1993 No 191).

The provisions governing the service of demand notices on a ratepayer are included within section 233 of the Local Government Act 1972; these are similar to those which were contained in section 109 of the General Rate Act 1967. The demand notice may properly be issued under section 233 in a number of ways: with regard to an individual ratepayer, a body corporate (e.g. a limited company) or a partnership, the demand notice may be delivered, or sent by post or be left at a designated address. In the case of a trust, it can be served on one of the trustees. Service can also be effected by fixing the notice on a conspicuous part of the hereditament. In addition, the regulations allow for the notice to be sent or left at the hereditament which is the place of business of the ratepayer.

The day on which the demand notice is issued is:

(i)   if the demand notice is served by being left or sent by post, the day on which it was so left or posted; or

(ii) in any other case, the day on which the bill was served.

In the case of service by post, the due date for payment of the first instalment or full amount of rates is calculated from the date of postage. The Interpretation Act 1889 applies to the question of whether or not service actually took place. If the demand notice is delivered late, in the normal course of events this does not affect the due date for payment. Where the ratepayer contends that the letter was never delivered, and can prove this, then service is deemed not to have been effected.

The regulations (SI 1989 No 1058) allow fourteen days to elapse before payment is due (instead of the ten days previously allowed) in order to ensure that the ratepayer has had a reasonable time to make the necessary payment arrangements, and to allow for the fact that the bill may take longer than normal to arrive.

With regard to Wales and the City of London, the following regulations contain similar provisions concerning the form, contents and validity of demand notices and the supply of information to billing authorities:

● Non-Domestic Rating (Demand Notices) (Wales) Regulations 1993 (SI 1993 No 252);

● Community Charges and Non-Domestic Rating (Demand Notices) (City of London) Regulations 1992 (SI 1992 No 209).

(b) Methods of payment

Under Schedule 1 to the principal regulations (SI 1989 No 1058), the ratepayer has a statutory right to pay by ten equal instalments (see below). Other arrangements for the mode of payment are possible and are at the discretion of the billing authority; they can include a lump sum of the whole amount due, two half-yearly payments, or by less frequent or more frequent payments than are provided for under the statutory scheme. These alternative arrangements must be agreed in writing between the ratepayer and the billing authority (reg 7(3) SI 1989 No 1058).

(i) Statutory instalment scheme

The regulations introduced a statutory instalment scheme under which rates can be paid in equal instalments. Details of the instalments and the times at which they are to be paid must be printed on the bill. The regulations provide that where the demand notice is issued before 31 December in the relevant year, the number of instalments will be ten, or, if less, the number of whole months remaining in the year, less one. The instalments must be paid in the months specified in the notice, and on such day as is specified. Where the demand notice is issued between 1 January and 31 March in the relevant year, rates must be paid in a single instalment.

The regulations prescribe that where the amount due is less than £100, the billing authority may require payment in a single instalment. Where the amount due is greater than £100, the billing authority may require payment in instalments greater than £50. In those cases where the total amount to be paid is indivisible by the number of instalments, the amount due is divided by the number of instalments, and then rounded up or down to the nearest pound. The first instalment is then balanced to ensure that the total equals the rates payable. For example if the rates bill is £523 payable in eight instalments, the first instalment will be £68, and the remaining seven instalments will each be £65.

The instalment facilities must be offered as of right to ratepayers: however, the billing authority and the ratepayer may enter into an agreement whereby the rates are paid in some other number of instalments. This procedure depends upon whether the billing authority intends to implement a flexible policy, given the fact that the authority's intention is to maximise cash flow and minimise arrears.

The statutory default provisions outlined in the regulations apply only where the ratepayer has failed to pay an instalment under the prescribed scheme (see below). As regards agreements outside the prescribed scheme, billing authorities will have to incorporate similar default provisions. It is important to bear in mind that where there is an agreement, the whole of the outstanding rates will become due on default only if the agreement provides for that. Once the sum has become due, the normal enforcement procedures come into operation.

With regard to part-year liability, the amount due is calculated on a daily basis. Circumstances can arise during the financial year which might result in a change of liability:

- a new building becomes capable of occupation (subject to the rules regarding empty property rates);
- a period of exemption from rates ends (e.g. enterprise zone properties);
- the occupation of a non-domestic property;
- the status of a property changes from domestic to non-domestic.

116

Where a ratepayer ceases to own or occupy a hereditament, the ratepayer's liability to rates ceases at the end of the previous day. The billing authority calculates the amount paid on a daily basis from 1 April to the date on which the liability ceased. If the amount payable is less than the total amount already due, the instalments will be adjusted accordingly. If the ratepayer has paid too much, the overpayment must be repaid.

If the liability of a ratepayer changes during the year, for example as a result of an alteration to the rating list, the charging authority must send the ratepayer a notice which adjusts the original bill and specifies the new instalments payable under it.

(ii) Failure to pay instalments

Under the statutory instalment scheme, when a ratepayer fails to pay an instalment, the billing authority must serve a further notice stating the amount required to be paid in order to bring the instalments up to date. If payment of the instalment is not made within seven days of the service of the notice, the right to pay by instalments is lost immediately, and the ratepayer is then under an obligation to pay the full amount of outstanding rates within the next seven days. If at the expiry of this second period the ratepayer is still in default, the authority can commence recovery proceedings by applying to the magistrates' court for a liability order. No further reminder notice is required to be served before recovery action is taken.

If the instalment is paid within the seven days, but the ratepayer defaults again later in the same year, the right to pay by instalments automatically ceases on the day of the default without the authority having to send a second notice. The ratepayer then has seven days to pay the full amount due. If no payment is made within the prescribed period, recovery proceedings can be implemented. In this case, however, if the authority decides to seek a liability order it must first serve a reminder notice notifying the ratepayer that such an order is being sought and giving him a further seven days to pay the full amount.

4. Enforcement

(a) Liability orders

A liability order is obtained by application to the magistrates' court (SI 1989 No 1058); it gives the billing authority the following enforcement powers:

Timetable for action

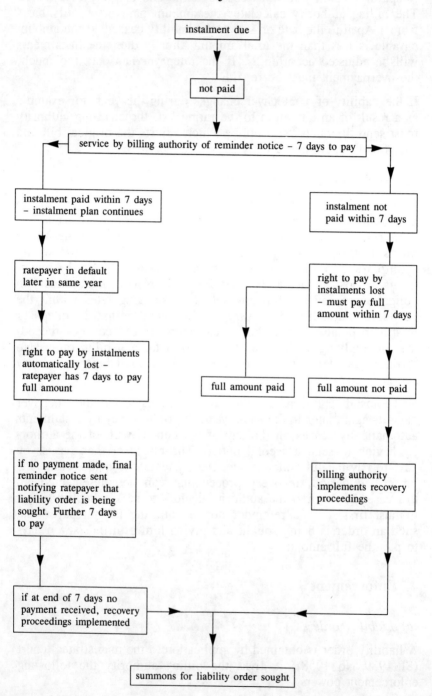

```
                    ┌──────────────────┐
                    │  instalment due  │
                    └──────────────────┘
                              │
                    ┌──────────────────┐
                    │     not paid     │
                    └──────────────────┘
                              │
    ┌─────────────────────────────────────────────────────────────┐
    │ service by billing authority of reminder notice – 7 days to pay │
    └─────────────────────────────────────────────────────────────┘
```

instalment due

not paid

service by billing authority of reminder notice – 7 days to pay

instalment paid within 7 days – instalment plan continues

instalment not paid within 7 days

ratepayer in default later in same year

right to pay by instalments lost – must pay full amount within 7 days

right to pay by instalments automatically lost – ratepayer has 7 days to pay full amount

full amount paid

full amount not paid

if no payment made, final reminder notice sent notifying ratepayer that liability order is being sought. Further 7 days to pay

billing authority implements recovery proceedings

if at end of 7 days no payment received, recovery proceedings implemented

summons for liability order sought

(i)   distress of goods; or

(ii) insolvency.

The billing authority will choose the power which it considers is best suited to the particular facts of each case. Where there is more than one owner or occupier, they will be jointly and severally liable for the amount outstanding and enforcement proceedings can be taken against any or all of them. But only one method of enforcement can be used against any one person at any time.

To obtain a liability order, it is necessary for the billing authority to lay a complaint before the magistrates. A summons is then served on the defaulter by (a) delivering it to him, or (b) sending it by post, or (c) leaving it at his place of abode or registered office.

At the hearing, if the magistrates are satisfied that the rates are payable and have not been paid, and that the relevant notices have been issued a liability order will be granted to the authority, irrespective of whether or not the debtor appears at the hearing. Defences available to the ratepayer against an issue of a liability order include:

- the property in respect of the unpaid rates did not appear in the local rating list for the relevant period;
- the prescribed provisions relating to notices and reminders were not adhered to;
- the amount due has been paid;
- the amount due has been incorrectly calculated;
- a person who is alleged to be jointly and severally liable was not in a relationship with the defaulting ratepayer at the time of the default.

Such matters as appeals against valuations, and exemptions from rates, are not a valid defence against the issue of a liability order.

As an alternative to applying for a liability order, the billing authority may seek to recover the sum payable in a court of competent jurisdiction.

Provision has been made to allow any person who was a party to the magistrates' courts proceedings, or who is aggrieved by the court's decision, to question those proceedings by way of case stated on the grounds that the court erred on a point of law or exceeded its jurisdiction. An appeal against the magistrates' court's decision must be made within twenty-one days of that decision.

(b) Distress

The provisions and procedures for distress are similar to those which operated under the General Rate Act 1967. The amount which can be recovered by way of distress and sale of the debtor's goods will be specified in the liability order together with any charges (which are prescribed in the regulations) associated with the distress. If the debtor pays the outstanding amount before any goods are seized, the authority is obliged to accept the amount and cease proceedings; if the goods have been seized and not yet sold, the authority must cease proceedings and make the goods available for collection.

With regard to resisting an application for a distress warrant, Browne LJ in *Camden London Borough Council v Herwald* [1978] QB 626 made the following comment:

'It is well established that an application for a distress warrant to enforce payment of rates can only be resisted on certain limited grounds. It is also well established that one of such grounds is that the defendant is not in occupation of the hereditament in respect of which it is sought to rate him.'

(See also *Associated Cinema Properties Ltd v Hampstead Borough Council* [1944] KB 412.)

The person levying the distress must carry written authorisation from the billing authority; in addition he must give the debtor a copy of regulation 14 and Schedule 3 of the main regulations (SI 1989 No 1058) which contain the provisions governing distress. Only the goods and chattels of the person named in the distress warrant can be distrained. Care must therefore be taken to ensure that the goods seized are the property of the defaulter. This point was to some extent relevant in *Re Els; Ramsbottom and Benzie v Luton Borough Council and Wrekin District Council* [1994] RA 363. In this case it was found that the crystallisation of a bank's floating charge completed the assignment of a company's goods to the bank, with the consequence that the goods subject to the distraint were no longer the goods of the company. Regulation 14 of the Non-Domestic Rating (Collection and Enforcement) (Local Lists) Regulations 1989 (SI 1989 No 1058) provided that 'where a liability order has been made, the authority which applied for the order may levy the appropriate amount by distress and sale of the goods of the debtor against whom the order was made'. It was the phrase 'goods of the debtor' which led to the High Court to conclude that distress was prevented by the crystallisation of the floating charge.

In the case of persons jointly and severally liable, distress cannot be levied against more than one person for the same outstanding debt at the same time. The regulations (SI 1990 No 145) include provisions to deal with enforcement action against partnerships, by allowing a liability order to be made in the name of the firm, as if orders had been made against each partner for the amount concerned (reg 5). In this case if distress is levied against the partnership property, the partners will be treated as jointly and severally liable for the charges incurred. Any person who is aggrieved by the levy of distress may appeal to the magistrates' court. If the court is satisfied that the levy was irregular, it may order those goods which have been distrained to be discharged if they are still in the possession of the billing authority. If any of the distrained goods have already been sold, the court can award compensation by way of special damages on the basis that proceedings could have been brought in trespass. An appeal against excessive distress may be made to the county court rather than the magistrates' court. See *Steel Linings Ltd v Bibby & Co* [1993] RA 27. In this case a liability order in respect of unpaid non-domestic rates in the sum of £9,869 was levied on the plaintiffs. The plaintiffs issued proceedings in the county court, complaining that the distress was excessive, in that industrial equipment worth £46,346 had been seized, and obtained an *ex parte* interlocutory injunction restraining the bailiffs from selling or disposing of the goods seized. The bailiffs appealed, contending that the county court had no jurisdiction to grant such an injunction. The Court of Appeal held that the statutory scheme for appeals to magistrates' courts in the Non-Domestic Rating (Collection and Enforcement) (Local Lists) Regulations 1989 (SI 1989 No 1058) did not oust the general jurisdiction of the county court to grant injunctions restraining the sale of goods seized or to order the return of those goods. However, the Court of Appeal made the point that, in order to succeed, the defaulting ratepayer would need to present a powerful *prima facie* case for saying that the distress had in some way been unlawful.

Distress may be levied anywhere in England and Wales, but may not be levied in Scotland.

(c) Committal to prison

In the light of recent court cases the Magistrates' Association has issued guidance in respect of applications to commit for non-payment of the community charge. The same principles should apply to cases concerning non-payment of non-domestic rates. It has been suggested that it is advisable for magistrates to enquire at the outset of a case as to whether other methods of recovery have been attempted. In *R v Highbury Corner Magistrates' Court, ex parte Uchendu* [1994] RA 51, an order of a magistrates' court committing a debtor to prison for three months was quashed by the High Court. Laws J made the following important point:

> 'It is important too that [the magistrates] should have the principle of proportionality in mind while of course adhering to what is now well known law, namely that the purpose of exercising these powers is indeed not to extract retributive punishment but to encourage payment.'

The regulations provide that in those cases where distress has been levied, and it is found that there are no (or insufficient) goods on which to levy the amount, the authority can apply to the magistrates' court for a warrant committing the debtor to prison. Before issuing a warrant, the court must be satisfied that failure to pay is due to a person's wilful refusal or culpable neglect. The form of the warrant is prescribed in the regulations and may be executed anywhere in England and Wales. An option open to the court is to issue a suspended committal order; this normally includes an arrangement to pay.

The warrant will be made in respect of the amount for which the liability order is made, together with an amount to cover all other ancillary charges. The maximum period of imprisonment is three months, but there is provision for the term to be reduced proportionately if part or all of the outstanding debt is paid.

(d) Insolvency

Where a liability order has been obtained, and the debtor is an individual, the amount due is deemed to be a debt for the purposes of bankruptcy proceedings under the Insolvency Act 1986. Where the debtor is a company, winding-up proceedings can be implemented. Where a company is already in receivership, however, the courts can refuse to grant a winding-up order. In *Re Leigh Estates (UK) Ltd* [1994] RA 57, the council's petition for the winding up of the company in receivership in respect of unoccupied rates on a property owned by the company was dismissed because, as the council claimed, following a winding-up order it could recover rates from the receivers. The reason for seeking to wind up the company was not to improve the lot of unsecured creditors but rather to gain for itself a preferential status such as formerly attached to rates but which was removed by the Insolvency Act 1986.

If bankruptcy or winding-up proceedings are brought, no other recovery action can be taken. This does not affect the ratepayer's continuing rate liability.

Where a receiver has been appointed under the provisions of the Law of Property Act 1925, the receiver has a discretionary power to make a payment of rates. A receiver in occupation of a company's premises is normally deemed to be an agent of the company (s 109 Law of Property Act 1925); therefore rateable occupation remains that of the company, and is not vested in the receiver. Where a company does not give up possession, the appointment of a receiver does not constitute a change in occupation. In the House of Lords case of *Holywell Union and Halkyn Parish v Halkyn Drainage Co* [1895] AC 117, it was stated:

> 'The question of whether a person is an occupier or not within the rating law is a question of fact and does not depend upon legal title.'

Ratford and Hayward v Northavon District Council [1987] QB 357, [1986] 3 WLR 771 supports the contention that the receiver normally occupies the premises as an agent, and is not personally liable for rates. Although this was a decision under the General Rate Act 1967, it is reasonable to assume that the liability for receivers will remain broadly the same under the new statutes and regulations, but see *Re Sobam BV and Satelscoop BV* [1995] ECGS 189. A Scottish case, *McKillop and Watters* [1994] RVR 124, also demonstrates within that jurisdiction that receivers are not personally liable to pay rates in respect of the occupation of property owned by a company in receivership.

Where the billing authority is unable to recover rates as an expense of the receivership, or by making the receiver personally liable, it can consider the option of distress following the making of a liability order.

Where a bankruptcy order has been made, the bankrupt's estate becomes subject to the Insolvency Act 1986. In effect unsecured creditors, unless preferred or deferred, rank equally (s 328(3) Insolvency Act 1986). To ensure that the bankrupt's estate remains available for distribution amongst creditors, the Insolvency Act provides for the vesting of the estate in the trustee.

Where a liability order has been made, any sum outstanding at the commencement of the bankruptcy (i.e. the making of the bankruptcy order) is a bankruptcy debt. The debt under the liability order is treated as an ordinary unsecured debt.

(e) Outstanding liabilities on death

Where a ratepayer dies, the executor or administrator must make any payments which are outstanding or would have become due.

Any sums payable by the executor or administrator are enforceable against him only in his capacity as such, as a debt of the deceased. No liability order need be sought.

5. Central lists

The requirements for collection and enforcement under the central non-domestic rating lists are essentially similar to those for the local rating lists. It is the responsibility of the Secretary of State to serve the demand notice, which may be given or served:

(a) in the case of an individual, by delivering it to him, or by leaving it at, or by sending it by post to him at his last known place of abode;

(b) in the case of a body corporate, by addressing it to the secretary of the body, by delivering it to him, or by leaving it at, or by sending it by post to him at the registered or principal office of the body;

(c) by leaving it at, or by sending it by post to the person at an address given by the person as an address at which service of the notice will be accepted.

(a) Demand notices

The Secretary of State must serve a demand notice for each chargeable financial year on every person who is a ratepayer and must serve a different demand notice for different chargeable years.

The demand notice must specify the amount of rates due for the whole or part of the chargeable year. Unless there is an agreement between the ratepayer and the Secretary of State, payment is required in instalments. Although this principle applies also to local rating lists, ratepayers under central lists have greater flexibility with regard to agreements made with the Secretary of State; in addition such agreements may be made after the issue of the demand notice.

(b) Failure to pay

If an instalment which is due has not yet been paid, the Secretary of State must serve a further notice on the ratepayers, specifying the instalment required to be paid and giving a period of seven days within which it must be paid. If the ratepayer fails to pay within the allotted period, the Secretary of State can take recovery proceedings.

Chapter 10

Relief from rates

Relevant legislation:

- Local Government Finance Act 1988;
- Non-Domestic Rating (Discretionary Relief) Regulations 1989 (SI 1989 No 1059);
- Non-Domestic Rating Contributions (England) Regulations 1989 (SI 1989 No 2435).

1. Introduction

Charitable and other organisations have been given a privileged position as regards liability to and relief from rates. Under section 40 of the General Rate Act 1967, rating authorities were empowered to grant two types of relief:

- mandatory relief (of 50 per cent); and
- discretionary relief (of up to 100 per cent).

Although both reliefs remain available under the new system, there have been some important changes effected by the LGFA 1988 which are detailed below.

Additionally, section 53 and paragraph 3A of Schedule 1 to the General Rate Act 1967 empowered authorities to reduce or remit rates on the grounds of poverty or hardship, although the former terms was not thought appropriate to other than householders.

2. Mandatory relief

As mentioned above, mandatory relief under the General Rate Act 1967 was at 50 per cent; under the LGFA 1988, this level has been increased to 80 per cent. In other words, the maximum rates payable are one-fifth of the normal rates (s 43(5) LGFA 1988). Relief applies where the ratepayer is a charity – or trustees for a charity – and the hereditament, if occupied, is wholly or mainly used for charitable purposes either of that charity or of that and other charities (s 43(6) LGFA 1988).

In addition, a billing authority can remit the remaining 20 per cent of rates under its discretionary powers (see below). An important change to the previous system is that it is no longer necessary for the charity to apply for mandatory relief – this should be given automatically. As regards the discretionary relief of the remaining 20 per cent, whether relief can be given will depend upon the rules established by each billing authority.

3. Discretionary relief

Under powers conferred by section 47 of the LGFA 1988, a billing authority can grant up to 100 per cent relief with respect to the following:

(a) any hereditament which has been given mandatory relief of 80 per cent;

(b) any hereditament occupied by an institution or organisation not established or conducted for profit and whose main objects are charitable or are otherwise philanthropic or religious or concerned with education, social welfare, science, literature or the fine arts;

(c) any hereditament wholly or mainly used for purposes of recreation, and all or part of it is occupied for the purposes of a club, society or other organisation not established or conducted for profit.

There is no formal procedure laid down in the regulations governing application for relief. A billing authority should bear in mind the following:

(i) Each billing authority should establish its own rules and criteria for deciding whether or not to grant relief, and the level of that relief. It is suggested that each case should be looked at on its own merits; the operation of a blanket decision to refuse relief could be construed as *ultra vires* and lead to litigation.

(ii) In deserving cases, billing authorities should take the initiative and grant relief before any application by the body or organisation is made (there is no statutory requirement for any application to be made).

(iii) Where an application for relief has been unsuccessful, the billing authority should state its reasons for refusal; this in certain cases could allow the organisation to conform to the criteria for relief.

4. Criteria

The following are examples of some of the 'tests' which it has been suggested a billing authority might wish to adopt in deciding whether to grant relief and in determining the level of that relief:

(a) Access

Is membership of the organisation open to the whole community, or are there rules of barriers to membership? If so, are they reasonable? For example, requirements that members should possess a certain level of technical skill may be acceptable, but very high fees are probably unacceptable.

Is there active encouragement of membership from sections of the community which the authority considers particularly deserving?

Also, is there a wider use of facilities than just the immediate membership?

(b) Provision of facilities

Self-help for construction or maintenance may be a useful indication of being deserving of relief, as is the past application of grant aid. Another useful indicator is if the provision of facilities saves the authority from having to provide them, or at least complements or supplements those provided. Finally, the mere presence of a bar should no longer automatically exclude relief – as happened in the past in some parts of the country.

* * *

Other valid considerations may be whether the catchment area for the organisation's membership is predominantly in the charging authority's area and whether the organisation is actively involved in national or local development of their interests by being affiliated to local or national organisations.

In the interest of good public relations, as well as natural justice, it is desirable that the authority publishes the general basis and specific criteria on which it will consider the merits of specific applications for discretionary relief.

At any stage a billing authority can revoke or amend its decisions and/or rules. Simply complying with the billing authority's rules is not sufficient to obtain relief; the billing authority must have taken a decision to apply relief to the hereditament concerned (s 47(3) LGFA 1988). The Regulations (SI 1989 No 1059) deal with the period of which relief may be granted, and the notice which should be used for any variation or termination of relief.

An aggrieved organisation can apply for judicial review of any decision of the billing authority which was made in the exercise of its discretion to grant relief. However, if the billing authority properly applied itself to the rules established, and did not reach a decision which no reasonable authority could have made, the court is likely to find in favour of the authority.

5. Unoccupied rates

Charities are liable to pay one-fifth of unoccupied rates (s 45(5)). Billing authorities have the power to remit unoccupied rates, provided that the hereditament is likely to be wholly or mainly used for charitable or recreational purposes when next in use (s 48 LGFA 1988). Where a charity is liable for unoccupied rates, the provisions regarding phasing will apply, as prescribed under the Non-Domestic Rating (Transitional Period) Regulations 1990 (SI 1990 No 608) (as amended).

6. Transitional arrangements

Charities are subject to the transitional arrangements on that part of the rates bill which they are required to pay. In other words, charities are liable to pay one-fifth of the ordinary rates after taking phasing into account.

7. Financial implications

The financial implications of an authority's decision to grant relief are determined by the Non-Domestic Rating Contributions (England) Regulations 1989 (SI 1989 No 2435), with similar regulations for Wales. With regard to *mandatory* relief, the regulations provide for the full cost of mandatory relief to charities to be borne by the non-domestic rate pool. If a billing authority exercises its discretion to grant relief at a level higher than the mandatory level, the regulations provide that 25 per cent of the balance of the relief granted can be set off against the non-domestic rate pool, leaving the remaining 75 per cent to be borne by the Council taxpayers. With regard to *discretionary* relief, the cost of any discretionary relief granted is split as follows: 75 per cent is borne by the non-domestic rate pool, and the remaining 25 per cent is borne by the Council taxpayers.

8. Hardship

Section 17 and Schedule 1 to the General Rate Act 1967 enabled a rating authority to charge rates on unoccupied property. In its original form, Schedule 1 limited the amount payable by an owner to one half of the amount which would have been payable if he were in occupation of the hereditament. That limitation was removed by the Local Government Act 1974, and was replaced by a provision which enabled the rating authority to fix the percentage payable. Thus from 1974 onwards the owner of a vacant building might find himself liable to pay the same rates as if the building were occupied. It was realised, however, that this might create hardship for the owner, and therefore a new paragraph 3A was inserted into Schedule 1 to the General Rate Act 1967.

In the consultation paper, *Paying for Local Government*, it was argued that the power to remit rates should cease. Due to the pressure on the Government, however, the Finance Bill 1988 was amended to include provision for the reduction or remission of liability to both occupied and unoccupied rates. Section 49 of the LGFA 1988 contains the current provisions. Three-quarters of the cost of any reduction or remittance of rates can be offset against an authority's payment into the national non-domestic rate pool; the remaining quarter must be borne locally. The amount of reduction or remission made to a ratepayer must reflect any other discretionary reliefs that he is entitled to, so as to avoid double relief.

Essentially, the billing authority has a discretionary power either to reduce the unoccupied rate or to remit the whole amount. However, the authority can exercise its discretion only if it is satisfied on both of the following points:

(a) the ratepayer would sustain hardship if the authority did not act; and

(b) it is reasonable for the authority to do so, having regard to the interests of persons subject to its Council tax, for example where the employment prospects in the area would be worsened if a company closed down.

(a) The ratepayer would sustain hardship if the authority did not act

The term 'hardship' is not confined to financial hardship: all circumstances should be considered in judging whether the payment of rates will cause hardship. Hardship need not be regarded as relating solely to private individuals; it can also apply to commercial companies or corporate bodies (see Circular No 34/78).

A number of cases have considered the authority's duty to exercise its discretion to rates relief. In *R v Liverpool City Council, ex parte Caplin* (1984) 24 RVR 132, the Queen's Bench Division held that a rating authority's refusal to grant relief from unoccupied rates on the ground of hardship was not unreasonable. This was because the hardship resulted from the improvident actions of the ratepayer. In brief, the ratepayers had purchased a property which was producing no income, and the purchase had been wholly financed with borrowed money. It was concluded that the applicants knew or ought to have known that they would be liable for rates until tenants could be found.

In *R v Liverpool City Council, ex parte Windsor Securities Ltd* [1979] RA 159, the ratepayers acquired a rambling office building in which there were fifty-two separate occupations; the intention of the ratepayers was to demolish the building and redevelop the site. Difficulties occurred when they attempted to obtain vacant possession. The rating authority resolved to levy unoccupied rates, and the ratepayers then applied for relief of rates on the ground of hardship. The application was turned down by the authority; the ratepayers then appealed to the Queen's Bench Division on the grounds that the authority had misconstrued the purpose of the hardship provisions and had failed to act fairly and to observe the rules of natural justice. The Divisional Court found for the authority, and the ratepayers then appealed to the Court of Appeal which found that the application for relief had been validly considered by the rating authority.

In *Wakefield Metropolitan District Council v Huzminor Investment Developments Ltd* [1989] RVR 108, one of the questions before the court was 'what constitutes hardship for a commercial company for the purpose of remission of rates otherwise due'. The court found the best answer to this in the judgment of Cumming-Bruce LJ in the *Windsor Securities* case: 'The question whether payment would cause hardship to these applicants has to be resolved in the light of common sense having regard to all the circumstances'. In the *Wakefield* case, the company had sought remission of a sum of £4,000 on the grounds of hardship, but the authority had refused to grant relief. The judgment of the High Court was that the company would not suffer any hardship. This was based on its view of the financial circumstances of the company, including the fact that the company had reserves of around £27,000, and was able to pay its directors a fee of £18,000 for management services and still make a profit of £411.

In *Investors in Industry Commercial Properties Ltd v Norwich City Council* [1986] AC 822, [1986] 2 WLR 925, the ratepayers were the owners of a new hereditament which had been completed in 1976, and since its completion had remained wholly or partly unoccupied. They became liable to unoccupied rates to the amount of £224,000. The issue was whether the ratepayers were entitled to appeal to the Crown Court with regard to a rating authority's exercise or failure to exercise its discretion to reduce or remit payment of rates on grounds of hardship. The House of Lords decided that the Crown Court was an appropriate tribunal to hear appeals against a rating authority's administrative decisions.

(b) It is reasonable for the authority to exercise its discretion

The authority must consider what effect the grant of relief would have on the level of its Council Tax. In essence the authority is required to weigh up the benefit to the ratepayer seeking remission or reduction with the potential increased cost to Council taxpayers. Before any decision can be taken, it would seem prudent that the authority should seek further information such as company accounts detailing losses, reserves of the company and the extent of any hardship.

One type of property which could benefit from the targeting of hardship relief is the small village store or sub-post office, if the retention of these businesses would be to the benefit of the local community. But again it should be remembered that a reduction can only be made if the ratepayer would sustain hardship in paying the non-domestic rates.

If the authority exercises its discretion and agrees to a reduction, the reduction is effective from the start of the financial year in which the application is made, and is reviewed annually. Relief would obviously be withdrawn on the sale of the business.

It should be borne in mind that the billing authority's right to grant a reduction or to remit rates on unoccupied property is entirely at its discretion. The application of this discretionary right is open to legal redress in the Crown Court and higher courts; therefore the authority must ensure that in deciding a case it has acted on all the information before it, and that it has not acted in such a manner as to frustrate the object and purpose of the statute conferring the power.

Appendix

Specimen forms

Contents

1. Form VO 7009: Notice of deletion of an existing 1995 Rating List entry

Dear *

THIS NOTICE IS IMPORTANT

NOTICE OF DELETION OF AN EXISTING 1995 RATING LIST ENTRY

I have now deleted from the Rating List the entry shown below :-

Billing Authority :	*
Reference Number :	*
Description :	*
Rateable Value :	£*
Effective date of deletion of entry :	*
Actual date of Alteration :	*
Address :	*

An entry in the Rating List indicates liability for the payment of rates for each day it appears in the list. This liability has now ended. You may appeal against the deletion and the effective date shown above even if you have an earlier appeal outstanding.

If you wish to appeal you can obtain a proposal form from this office. Enquiries about the payment of rates should be directed to the Billing Authority. For any other queries please contact this office, quoting "Our reference" shown above.

Yours faithfully

*

Valuation Officer

VO 7009 (1995)

2. Form VO 7010: Notice of alteration to the 1995 Rating List

Dear *

THIS NOTICE IS IMPORTANT

NOTICE OF ALTERATION TO THE 1995 RATING LIST

I have now made a new entry in the Rating List as follows :-

Billing Authority :	*
Reference Number :	*
Description :	*
Rateable Value :	£*
Effective date of Alteration :	*
Actual date of Alteration :	*
Address :	*

An entry in the Rating List indicates liability for the payment of rates. You may appeal against any aspect of the new entry even if you have an earlier appeal outstanding.

If you wish to appeal, you can obtain a proposal form from this office.

Enquiries about the payment of rates should be directed to the Billing Authority. For any other queries please contact this office, quoting "Our reference" shown above.

Yours faithfully

*

Valuation Officer

Enc.

VO 7010 (1995)

3. Form VO 7011a: Notice of alteration to an existing 1995 Rating List entry (as a result of alterations to the property)

Dear *

THIS NOTICE IS IMPORTANT

NOTICE OF ALTERATION TO AN EXISTING 1995 RATING LIST ENTRY

I have now altered the Rating List as follows :-

Billing Authority : *
Reference Number : *
Description : *
Rateable Value : £*
Effective date of Alteration : *
Actual date of Alteration : *
Address : *

An entry in the Rating List indicates liability for the payment of rates. You may appeal against any aspect of the new entry even if you have an earlier appeal outstanding.

If you wish to appeal you can obtain a proposal form from this office.

FOR YOUR INFORMATION
The previous List entry was : Rateable Value :   £*
The reason for this notice is that alterations have been made to the property, and the previous assessment is now considered to be incorrect.

Enquiries about the payment of rates should be directed to the Billing Authority. For any other queries please contact this office, quoting "Our reference" shown above.

Yours faithfully

*

Valuation Officer

Enc.

VO 7011a (1995)

4. Form VO 7011b: Notice of alteration to an existing 1995 Rating List entry (previous assessment incorrect)

Dear *

THIS NOTICE IS IMPORTANT

NOTICE OF ALTERATION TO AN EXISTING 1995 RATING LIST ENTRY

I have now altered the Rating List as follows :-

Billing Authority :	*
Reference Number :	*
Description :	*
Rateable Value :	£*
Effective date of Alteration :	*
Actual date of Alteration :	*
Address :	*

An entry in the Rating List indicates liability for the payment of rates. You may appeal against any aspect of the new entry even if you have an earlier appeal outstanding.

If you wish to appeal you can obtain a proposal form from this office.

FOR YOUR INFORMATION
The previous List entry was : Rateable Value : £*
The reason for this notice is the previous assessment was incorrect.

Enquiries about the payment of rates should be directed to the Billing Authority. For any other queries please contact this office, quoting "Our reference" shown above.

Yours faithfully

*

Valuation Officer

Enc.

VO 7011b (1995)

5. Form VO 7012: Proposal to alter the 1995 Rating List

PROPOSAL
Valua ffice   ## TO ALTER THE
1995 RATING LIST

Please read the guidance notes for this form before completing .
Please write clearly using black ink. It is essential that all sections
are answered fully. Failure to do so may invalidate the Proposal.

This form should be returned to:-	RSA Case No.
	Case Type
	Date Received
	Section No.

PART A - DETAILS OF THE PROPERTY/RATING ASSESSMENT

Please enter below details of the property and where appropriate the Rating List entry to which this proposal relates. If more than one property or list entry is involved the additional details should be shown on a separate sheet of paper and attached to this form.

1 Address of property to which the proposal relates

Postcode

2 Description of the property to which the proposal relates

3 Name of the occupier

4 Address of the occupier (if different to 1)

Postcode

5 Rateable Value (please see note 5)

6 Effective date (please see note 6)

7 If the property is owner/occupied please tick
   If NOT then state the name of owner

8 Owners address (if different from 1 and 4)

Postcode

9 Billing Authority

10 Reference number (please see note 10)

PART B - DETAILS OF THE PROPOSED LIST ALTERATION

Please complete **11** or **12** as appropriate. (see guidance notes 11 and 12)

11 I propose that the Rating List entry shown for the above property (and those on the attached sheet) should be altered as follows: *(Note: please tick the relevant box(es) and supply additional information as necessary).*

A The Rateable Value increased to £ **with effect from**

B The Rateable Value reduced to £ **with effect from**

C The existing entry deleted **with effect from**

D The existing entry divided into *(insert number)* **with effect from**

E The existing entries *(insert number)* merged into one **with effect from**

F The effective date changed to

G Other changes
   (please specify)
   with effect from

or

12 I propose that the property identified in Part A above should be shown as a new entry
    in the Rating List at a Rateable Value of £ **with effect from**

VO 7012 (1995) *Please turn to page 2 and enter further details of your proposal.* *page 1.*

139

Reverse side of Form VO 7012

PART C - GROUNDS FOR YOUR PROPOSED ALTERATION

13 I have reason to believe that the Rating List is inaccurate and that the alteration proposed in PART B of this form should be made because:
TICK ONLY ONE BOX. If more than one of the following statements apply, select the one you consider most appropriate. Detailed reasons for believing that grounds A or D-K are applicable should be given at **14** below.

	A	The Rateable Value(s) in the Rating List as at 1 April 1995 was/were inaccurate	01
or	**B**	The alteration made by the Valuation Officer on was inaccurate	02
or	**C**	The effective date of the alteration made by the Valuation Officer on is inaccurate	03
or	**D**	Circumstances affecting the Rateable Value of the property changed on	04
or	**E**	The property has been demolished or no longer exists	05
or	**F**	The property is now domestic or exempt from rating and is no longer rateable	06
or	**G**	The entry shown should be deleted for reasons other than those at **E** and **F** above	07
or	**H**	The property should be shown as more than one assessment	08
or	**I**	The properties should be shown as one or more different assessments	09
or	**J**	I consider the property to be Rateable	10
or	**K**	The entry is wrong by reason of a decision dated	11

of the   *Valuation Tribunal/*Lands Tribunal/*High Court

in respect of the following property   *delete as appropriate*

Postcode

This decision is relevant to the Rating List entry of the property to which this proposal relates because

or	**L**	A statement required to be made in the List about the property is wrong or has been omitted.	12

14 My detailed reasons for believing that the Rating List is inaccurate are

PART D - DETAILS OF THE PERSON COMPLETING THIS PROPOSAL

15 Capacity in which this Proposal is made

Occupier   *Agent for* Occupier
Owner   *Agent for* Owner
Owner/Occupier   *Agent for* Owner/Occupier
Billing Authority *Agent for* Billing Authority
other capacity *Please state*

17 Address for correspondence

Postcode

18 Daytime telephone number

16 Name in CAPITAL LETTERS

19 FAX No.

Signed

20 Your Reference (if applicable)

Dated

page 2.

6. *Leaflet VO 7012a: Guidance notes for completion of a 'Proposal to alter the 1995 Rating List'*

PROPOSAL	**Guidance Notes**
TO ALTER THE	**for Completion**
1995 RATING LIST	PLEASE READ THESE NOTES CAREFULLY
	BEFORE COMPLETING THE FORM

If you have any queries about completing the form, or you have any other enquiries you wish to make, please telephone your local Valuation Office and a member of staff will be pleased to assist you. Further details about the Rating List and the Rating System are also available in a separate leaflet which can be obtained from any Valuation Office.
It is important that sufficient information about the property(ies) and the existing Rating List entry(ies) to which the proposal relates is supplied to enable accurate identification by the Valuation Officer. Failure to answer all sections fully may invalidate the proposal.
Where your Proposal relates to more than one property/entry please use the form for one of the properties and record details for the remaining property(ies)/entry(ies) on a separate sheet of paper which should then be attached to the Proposal from.

PART A - DETAILS OF THE PROPERTY/RATING ASSESSMENT

1 Enter the full address of the property as shown in the Rating List or that which you consider should be shown if you are proposing a new entry (see box 12). If the existing Rating List address is incorrect please also show here the correct full postal address (or in Section 14 of Part C if there is insufficient space)

2 Enter the description of the property (eg "Shop and premises"). This is shown in column 2 of the Rating List and on a Notice of Alteration issued by the Valuation Officer. It may also be shown on your rates bill

3 Enter the name of the present occupier of the property shown at 1 on the form.

4 The full postal address of the occupier of the property should be provided here if it is different from that shown at 1 on the form. Otherwise enter "as 1".

5 Enter the rateable value of the relevant assessment you disagree with. The rateable value is shown in column 5 of the Rating List and on a Notice of Alteration issued by the Valuation Officer. It is also shown on your rates bill.

6 Enter the effective date of the rating assessment you disagree with. This is the date from which a new or altered liability to rate payment starts. The date is shown in the Rating List and on a Notice of Alteration issued by the Valuation Officer. Please enter "1-4-95" if the proposal relates to the original entry shown in the Rating List.

7 If the property is occupied by the owner please tick the box "Owner/Occupier". If not, enter the name of the owner of the property in the space provided.

8 The full postal address of the owner should be entered if it is different from that shown for 1 and 4. Otherwise enter "as 1" or "as 4" as appropriate.

9 Please enter the name of the Billing Authority which collects rates on the property.

10 Enter the reference number of the assessment (if known), this is shown in column 1 of the Rating List and on a Notice of Alteration issued by the Valuation Officer. It may also be shown on your rates bill.

PART B - DETAILS OF THE PROPOSED LIST ALTERATION

This part of the Proposal form should be used to record the nature of the change to the Rating List that is being proposed. Please complete Section 11 if your Proposal relates to an existing Rating List entry or Section 12 if it is to include a new entry (ie one not currently shown in the List).

11 The series of tick boxes A to F identify many of the alterations that are commonly made. An additional box G allows for any "other change" to be recorded. **At least one of the boxes must be ticked** in order to ensure that the Proposal meets minimum validity requirements but additional boxes may also be ticked if appropriate. If you tick G it is necessary to specify exactly what change you propose. The date from which you consider the proposed change should take effect should also be entered in the space provided. Complete F if you are only disputing the Effective Date of an alteration that has been made to the Rating List by the Valuation Officer. If you are proposing an increase or reduction in rateable value it will be helpful if, in addition to ticking the relevant box (A or B), you also show the amount of rateable value you consider appropriate. The following examples are given to assist completion of this part of the form.

> *example 1*
> *if you are appealing because there has been a "material change of circumstances" (ie. a physical change in the property or the locality) you will need to indicate its effect upon the rateable value (by ticking either box A or B) and also enter in the adjoining "with effect from" box the date on which you believe the change occurred; (eg. 10 May 1995 should be entered as 10 05 95)*

> *example 2*
> *if you consider that the property is no longer rateable (eg a shop has ceased trading and has been converted to wholly domestic use) tick box C and show in the adjoining box the date you believe the change occurred.*

If you are seeking to make more than one alteration to the Rating List and each proposed alteration relates to different events in time please use a separate Proposal form for each event. For example, if you are (1) disputing a Rating List alteration made by the Valuation Officer on 1 May 1995 (to increase the rateable value) and (2) seeking a reduction on the grounds of a "material change of circumstances" that occurred on 10 December 1995, use separate Proposal forms for each proposed alteration to the List.

12 Complete this section only if your proposal is to show a new entry in the Rating List for the property identified in Part A.

VO 7012a GN (1995)

Reverse side of Form VO 7012a

PART C - GROUNDS FOR YOUR PROPOSED ALTERATION

13 Please **select the statement** that you consider best describes why you are proposing the alteration shown in Part B and then **tick the box** adjoining. **Tick only ONE of the boxes lettered A to L and supply such additional information** as necessary in the space provided - the following notes are provided to help you select the appropriate box to tick;

Box A if you think the Rateable Value(s) in the Rating List following the 1995 Revaluation was/were inaccurate.

Box B if you dispute the accuracy of an alteration made by the Valuation Officer. Please also enter in the space provided the date the alteration was made. NB this date is shown in the relevant Schedule of Alterations (held with the Rating List at the Billing Authority offices) and in the corresponding Notice of Alteration issued by the Valuation Officer. If you also disagree with the Effective Date of the alteration please ensure that the date which you consider correct has been entered in Section B under Section 11, F.

Box C if you are not disputing the accuracy of an assessment made by the Valuation Officer but disagree with its Effective Date and wish to replace it with the one you have shown at Section 11F of PART B. Please also enter in the space provided the date the alteration was made by the Valuation Officer.

Box D if you believe the rateable value is inaccurate because there has been a material change of circumstances (ie. a physical change to the property or the locality). The date the change of circumstances occurred should be entered in the space provided. (NB you should also have indicated the effect of the change on the rateable value in Section 11 of PART B).

Box E if you think the entry in the list should be deleted because the property has been demolished or no longer exists.

Box F if you believe the assessment should be deleted from the List because the property is now used wholly for residential purposes or is exempt from rating (eg it is now an agricultural building).

Box G if you think the entry in the list should be deleted for a reason other than 13E or 13F. (eg. an entry appears in the wrong Rating List as a result of a boundary change).

Box H if the property is currently shown in the Rating List as a single assessment and you consider that it should be shown as two or more assessments (ie it is occupied as two or more separate parts).

Box I if you consider that two or more existing assessments should be combined into a single or two or more different assessments in the Rating List (ie all the property is in the same occupation).

Box J if your proposal is to include in a Rating List a property that is currently not shown in that List.

Box K if you believe the entry shown in the List is wrong in the light of a Tribunal or Court decision relating to another property. You should enter the date of the decision, name of the tribunal/court and the address of the property to which the decision relates. **You must also provide your reasons for believing that the decision is relevant** to the Rating List entry to which your proposal relates (ie. that shown in part A).

Box L if you consider that the address, description or any other statement required by law to be made in the List about the property is wrong or has been omitted.

14 **This section should be used to provide your detailed reason(s) for believing the Rating List to be inaccurate if you have ticked any of the boxes 13A or D to K**

e.g. For box D, the reason might be that part of the property has been demolished, or, that a newly built property has been occupied by a competitor. For box K, the reason might be that a Tribunal reduced the assessment of a very similar property in the vicinity.

PLEASE NOTE *that all rateable values are based on the yearly rent at which a property might reasonably have been let on 1 April 1993. Any increase or fall resulting from general changes in the rental market since then will not affect its rateable value.*

PART D - DETAILS OF THE PERSON COMPLETING THIS PROPOSAL

Completion of this part of the form will help with communication between yourself, the Valuation Officer and any other parties who might be involved in your Proposal. It is recommended therefore that you complete this part as fully as possible.

15 Tick the box which indicates the capacity in which the Proposal is being made, ie that which most accurately describes your involvement. Please tick one box only. If you select "Other Capacity" please explain the nature of the capacity in which you have signed the form.

16 Please enter your name in capital letters. Your normal signature should be entered beneath and the form should also be dated.

PLEASE ENSURE THAT ALL APPROPRIATE SECTIONS HAVE BEEN COMPLETED BEFORE SIGNING THE FORM

17 Please enter the full postal address to which correspondence should be sent. However if this address has already been entered in full elsewhere on the form it is unnecessary to repeat it here. Instead please enter "As at section N" (where "N" is the printed number against the section of the form).

18 Please enter the telephone number at which you can normally be contacted during the day.

19 Your fax number should be entered here if you have one.

20 Complete this section with the reference (if any) that you would like quoted in future correspondence.

7. Form VO 7013: Notice of alteration to the 1995 Rating List for a reconstitution of an existing entry (i.e. splits or mergers)

Dear *

THIS NOTICE IS IMPORTANT

NOTICE OF ALTERATION TO THE 1995 RATING LIST

I have now made a new entry in the Rating List as follows :-

Billing Authority : *
Reference Number : *
Description : *
Rateable Value : £*
Effective date of Alteration : *
Actual date of Alteration : *
Address : *

An entry in the Rating List indicates liability for the payment of rates. You may appeal against any aspect of the new entry even if you have an earlier appeal outstanding.

If you wish to appeal you can obtain a proposal form from this office.

FOR YOUR INFORMATION
The coded reason for this notice is the property, or its occupation, has been rearranged to form a different rateable unit or units. The previous assessment will either have been divided into two or more assessments, or several assessments will have been merged. The previous assessment(s) *is *are listed.
(Where one previous assessment has been divided into several units the other assessments will be shown on separate Notices, issued to the occupiers or owners of those units.)

Enquiries about the payment of rates should be directed to the Billing Authority. For any other queries please contact this office, quoting "Our reference" shown above.

Yours faithfully

*

Valuation Officer

Enc

VO 7013 (1995)

8. Form VO 7044 (CL): Validity of proposal – appeal against Central Valuation Officer's decision

Central Valuation Officer
Room 175
New Court
Carey Street
LONDON   WC2A 2JE
Tel: 071 324 1175

Validity of Proposal -
Appeal Against Central Valuation Officer's Decision

Please write clearly using black ink.   ** Delete where not applicable*

Central Rating List for	
Assessment Number	
Designated Person to which the Proposal relates	
Description	

Date Proposal Made		Date of Central Valuation Officer's Notice	

I refer to your notice in which you state that, in your opinion, my proposal to alter the Central Rating List is not valid.

I hereby appeal against your decision for the reason(s) stated below *(continue overleaf if necessary)*

* I enclose copies of the following documents to support my appeal :-

Signed		Date	
Name			
Address for Correspondence			
		Postcode	
Daytime Telephone Number			

VO 7044 (CL)

9. Form VO 7044: Validity of proposal – appeal against Valuation Officer's decision

Valuation Office

Please send to:

1995 Rating List
Validity of Proposal -
Appeal Against Valuation Officer's Decision

* Delete if not appropriate   ***Please write clearly using black ink***

Billing Authority	
Reference Number	
Address of Property to which Proposal Relates	
	Postcode
Date Proposal Made	Date of Valuation Officer's Notice

I refer to your notice in which you state that, in your opinion, my proposal to alter the Rating List is not valid. I hereby appeal against your decision for the reason(s) stated below *(continue overleaf if necessary)*

* I enclose copies of the following documents to support my appeal :

Signed		Date
Name		
Address for Correspondence		
	Postcode	
Daytime telephone Number		

VO 7044 (1995) (6/95)   An Executive Agency of the Inland Revenue

145

10. Form VO 7058: Notice by interested person in respect of a proposal to alter the Rating List

Valuation Office

Please send to:

Notice by Interested Person
in respect of a
Proposal to alter the Rating List

Please write clearly using black ink

Billing Authority	
Assessment Number *(if appropriate)*	
Description *(if appropriate)*	
Address	
	Postcode
Proposal dated	
Made by	

To: The Valuation Officer

This notice is given in response to your letter dated [   ] in which you state that the proposal, referred to above, has been withdrawn.

As an interested person, I have to advise you that I wish to take part in the proceedings in respect of that proposal.

I confirm that I would have been entitled to make the proposal, in the same terms, on the day it was served on the Valuation Officer, in my capacity as * [   ] .

I understand that any alteration to the Rating List that may be made as a result of this notice shall have effect from the day that would have applied if the proposal had not been withdrawn.

Signed		Date	

Name (in CAPITALS please)	

Address for Correspondence		Daytime telephone number

* *Insert Occupier, Owner, Leaseholder, etc, as appropriate*

VO 7058

An Executive Agency of the Inland Revenue

11. Form VO 7300: Withdrawal of 1995 rating proposal/appeal

_____

*

Our Ref : *

Valuation Tribunal Serial No :
*

Date : *

_____

WITHDRAWAL OF 1995 RATING PROPOSAL

Billing Authority : *

Reference Number : *
Description : *
Address : *

The persons whose signatures are shown below agree that the proposal to alter the Rating List dated * made by * shall be withdrawn.
The persons whose signatures are shown below agree that the appeal made on * by * shall be withdrawn.

Signed by or on behalf of :-

1. **The proposer :**   _____

2. **The occupier at date of proposal :**   _____

3. **The ratepayer at date of agreement to withdraw :**   _____

4. **Any other interested person :**   _____
   (who has served notice on the Valuation Officer)
   ˏ
                                                         _____

5. **The Relevant Authority :**   _____

I confirm that all relevant parties of whom I am aware have signed this withdrawal.

Valuation Officer : _____   **Date :** _____

VO 7300 (1995)

12. Form VO 7300a: Withdrawal of 1995 rating proposal

---

*

Case No :   *

WITHDRAWAL OF 1995 RATING PROPOSAL

Billing Authority :   *

Reference Number :   *
Description :   *
Address :   *

The persons whose signatures are shown below agree that the proposal to alter the Rating List dated *
made by * shall be withdrawn.

Signed by or on behalf of :-

1. **The proposer :**

2. **The occupier at date of proposal :**

3. **The ratepayer at date of agreement to
    withdraw :**

4. **Any other interested person :**
    (who has served notice on the Valuation Officer)

5. **The Relevant Authority :**

I confirm that all relevant parties of whom I am aware have signed this withdrawal.

Valuation Officer : _____   Date : _____

13. Form VO 7300b: Withdrawal of 1995 rating appeal

*

Case No : *

Valuation Tribunal Serial No :
*

WITHDRAWAL OF 1995 RATING APPEAL

Billing Authority : *

Reference Number : *
Description : *
Address : *

The persons whose signatures are shown below agree that the appeal made on * by * shall be withdrawn.

Signed by or on behalf of :-

1. **The proposer :**   _____

2. **The occupier at date of proposal :**   _____

3. **The ratepayer at date of agreement to withdraw :**   _____

4. **Any other interested person :**   _____
   (who has served notice on the Valuation Officer)

   _____

5. **The Relevant Authority :**   _____

I confirm that all relevant parties of whom I am aware have signed this withdrawal.

Valuation Officer : _____ **Date :** _____

VO 7300b (1995)

14. Form VO 7302: Agreement to alter entry on value change

Case No : *
Valuation Tribunal Serial No : *

AGREEMENT TO ALTER THE 1995 RATING LIST

Billing Authority : *

This is an agreement to alter the Rating List in respect of a proposal dated * made by *.

The persons whose signatures appear on this document agree that the Rating List shall be altered by amending the existing entry to that shown below :-

Description : *
Rateable Value : £*
Effective date of Alteration : *
Address : *

Signed by or on behalf of :-

1. **The proposer :**

2. **The occupier at date of proposal :**
   (if different from 1 above)

3. **The ratepayer at date of agreement :**
   (if different from 1 and/or 2 above)

4. **Any other interested person :**
   (who has served notice on the Valuation Officer)

5. **The Relevant Authority :**
   (where appropriate)

6. **The Valuation Officer :**

   Date :

VO 7302 (1995)

150

15. Form VO 7303: Agreement to insert new entry

Case No :   *
Valuation Tribunal Serial No :   *

AGREEMENT TO ALTER THE 1995 RATING LIST

        Billing Authority :   *

This is an agreement to alter the Rating List in respect of a proposal dated * made by *.

The persons whose signatures appear on this document agree that the Rating List shall be altered by the insertion of the entry shown below :-

                      Description :   *
               Rateable Value :   £*
Effective date of Alteration :   *
                         Address :   *

Signed by or on behalf of :-

1.   **The proposer :**   _____

2.   **The occupier at date of proposal :**   _____
     (if different from 1 above)

3.   **The ratepayer at date of agreement :**   _____
     (if different from 1 and/or 2 above)

4.   **Any other interested person :**   _____
     (who has served notice on the Valuation Officer)

                                               _____

5.   **The Relevant Authority :**   _____
     (where appropriate)

6.   **The Valuation Officer :**   _____

     Date :   _____

VO 7303 (1995)

16. Form VO 7304: Agreement to delete an entry

Case No : *

Valuation Tribunal Serial No :   *

AGREEMENT TO ALTER THE 1995 RATING LIST

Billing Authority : *

This is an agreement to alter the Rating List in respect of a proposal dated * made by *.

The persons whose signatures appear on this document agree that the Rating List shall be altered by the deletion of the existing entry shown below, and the Effective Date of that alteration shall be as stated below :-

Reference Number : *
Description : *
Rateable Value : £*
Effective date in Rating List : *
Effective Date of Alteration : *
Address : *

Signed by or on behalf of :-

1. **The proposer :**   _____

2. **The occupier at date of proposal :**   _____
    (where appropriate)
    (if different from 1 above)

3. **The ratepayer at date of agreement :**   _____
    (where appropriate)
    (if different from 1 and/or 2 above)

4. **Any other interested person :**   _____
    (who has served notice on the Valuation Officer)

                                               _____

5. **The Relevant Authority :**   _____
    (where appropriate)

6. **The Valuation Officer :**   _____

    Date :   _____

17. Form VO 7305: Agreement for splits and mergers

Case No :   *
Valuation Tribunal Serial No :   *

AGREEMENT TO ALTER THE 1995 RATING LIST

    Billing Authority :   *

This is an agreement to alter the Rating List in respect of a proposal dated * made by *.

The persons whose signatures appear on this document agree that the Rating List shall be altered by the deletion of the existing entry(ies) shown and the insertion of the revised *entry *entries as shown on the schedule attached.

Signed by or on behalf of :-

1.   **The proposer :**   _____

2.   **The occupier*s at date of proposal :**   _____
     (if different from 1 above)

3.   **The ratepayer*s at date of agreement :**   _____
     (if different from 1 and/or 2 above)

4.   **Any other interested person*s :**   _____
     (who has served notice on the Valuation Officer)

                                               _____

5.   **The Relevant Authority :**   _____
     (where appropriate)

6.   **The Valuation Officer :**   _____

    Date :   _____

VO 7305 (1995)

Schedule attached to Form VO 7305

SCHEDULE FORMING PART OF AN AGREEMENT TO ALTER THE 1995 RATING LIST

Proposal dated * made by *

Ref	Description	Address	Rateable Value £	Effective Date in Rating List (if shown)	Effective Date of Alteration
1	2	3	4	5	6
<u>Existing Entry(ies)</u>					
*	*		*	*	*
<u>Revised Entry(ies)</u>					
*	*		*	*	*

VO 7305 (1995)

154

18. Form VO 7306: Agreement to alter former entry, i.e. historic entry

Case No : *
Valuation Tribunal Serial No : *

AGREEMENT TO ALTER THE 1995 RATING LIST

Billing Authority : *

This is an agreement to alter an entry previously shown in the Rating List which was the subject of a proposal dated * made by *.

The persons whose signatures appear on this document agree that the entry shown below shall be substituted for the relevant previous entry in the Rating List.

Reference Number : *
Description : *
Rateable Value : £*
Effective date of Alteration : *
Address : *

Signed by or on behalf of :-

1. **The proposer :** _____

2. **The occupier at date of proposal :** _____
   (if different from 1 above)

3. **The ratepayer at date of agreement :** _____
   (if different from 1 and/or 2 above)

4. **Any other interested person :** _____
   (who has served notice on the Valuation Officer)

   _____

5. **The Relevant Authority :** _____
   (where appropriate)

6. **The Valuation Officer :** _____

   Date : _____

VO 7306 (1995)

19. Form VO 7307: Agreement to alter former entry, i.e. historic entry for splits and mergers

Case No : *
Valuation Tribunal Serial No : *

AGREEMENT TO ALTER THE 1995 RATING LIST

Billing Authority : *

This is an agreement to alter *an entry *entries previously shown in the Rating List which *was *were the subject of a proposal dated * made by *.

The persons whose signatures appear on this document agree that for the *entry *entries previously shown in the Rating List shall be substituted for the revised *entry *entries which *is *are shown on the schedule attached.

Signed by or on behalf of :-

1. **The proposer :** _____

2. **The occupier*s at date of proposal :**   _____
   (if different from 1 above)

3. **The ratepayer*s at date of agreement :**   _____
   (if different from 1 and/or 2 above)

4. **Any other interested person*s :**   _____
   (who has served notice on the Valuation Officer)

   _____

5. **The Relevant Authority :**   _____
   (where appropriate)

6. **The Valuation Officer :**   _____

   Date :   _____

VO 7307 (1995)

Schedule attached to Form VO 7307

SCHEDULE FORMING PART OF AN AGREEMENT TO ALTER THE 1995 RATING LIST

Proposal dated * made by *.

Ref	Description	Address	Rateable Value £	Effective Date in Rating List (if shown)	Effective Date of Alteration
1	2	3	4	5	6
Existing Entry(ies)					
*	*	*	*	*	*
Revised Entry(ies)					
*	*	*	*	*	*

VO 7307 (1995)

Index

Standard Conditions of Sale
A conveyancer's guide
Fifth Edition

by Frances Silverman,
Solicitor and Reader in Law at the College of Law

This clear, easy-to-follow work looks at the requirements for a legally binding contract for the sale of land in England and Wales, providing a detailed commentary on the Standard Conditions of Sale which normally form the basis of the contract.

With its thorough and lucid analysis of the Conditions and logical format it will guide you easily through all your conveyancing problems:

- The Conditions are discussed in the order of events of a normal transaction, from service and delivery of documents to completion

- Each Condition is explained in the context of the general law

- Suggestions are provided for variations to each Condition, to cope with particular problems

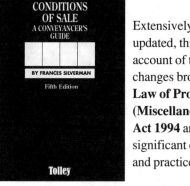

- For clarity and easy reference, Conditions which deal with particular circumstances such as leasehold property and sale of parts, are discussed in separate chapters towards the end of the book

Extensively revised and updated, this edition takes account of the sweeping changes brought about by the **Law of Property (Miscellaneous Provisions) Act 1994** and other significant changes in the law and practice.

The author is well-known for her authoritative, practical works on conveyancing and property law and has written this book with the everyday needs of solicitors, barristers, licensed conveyancers and other property professionals firmly in mind.

March 1996	280 pages approx	Order Code SCS5
ISBN 0 85459 162-4	Paperback	£39.95

MONEY-BACK GUARANTEE

*You can order **Standard Conditions of Sale** on 21 days approval. If you choose not to keep it, simply return it to us in a saleable condition within 21 days and we will refund your payment or cancel your invoice.*

How To Order

Standard Conditions of Sale is available through your local bookseller or by writing to:
Tolley Publishing Company Ltd., FREEPOST, Tolley House,
2 Addiscombe Road, Croydon, CR2 5WZ, or ring our order line
on 0181 686 9141 / Fax: 0181 686 3155.

Tolley